ETHICS IN FISCAL ADMINISTRATION

Ethics in Fiscal Administration: An Introduction integrates ethics into the public administration curriculum by weaving ethical dilemmas into the financial management and budgeting process of the public and nonprofit sectors. Inquiry-based discussion prompts challenge students to examine scenarios that they are likely to encounter in professional public service careers.

Critics of the public sector often use the analogy that government should be run more like a business. Issues such as profitability versus social value preclude the public sector from becoming a mirror image of the private sector; however, ethical decision making in fiscal administration is an important concern across sectors. Using examples drawn from the public and nonprofit arenas, *Ethics in Fiscal Administration: An Introduction* will help prepare future budget managers and other public administrators for the important work of upholding the public financial trust.

Angela Pool-Funai is Assistant Professor of Political Science and Public Administration, Director of the Master of Public Administration program, and interim Associate Dean of the College of Humanities and Social Sciences at Southern Utah University, USA.

"A book for any MPA course! Pool-Funai grapples with all the important moral and ethical issues facing public servants, integrating theories into modern decision making. Transparency. Whistle-blowing. Technology. Government versus Business. You name it; she offers a case scenario to prompt an extraordinary classroom discussion."

– **Patricia Keehley**, *Southern Utah University, USA*

"The author importantly presents an ethical framework that emphasizes the importance of transparency, participation, and collaboration in the public sector. Serious students and practitioners of public administration and fiscal policy should read this book as a catalyst for their own careers."

– **James Walter Peterson**, *Professor Emeritus, Valdosta State University, USA*

"Life is all about people. Dr. Pool-Funai's thought provoking work outlines the need of an ethical framework to ensure we can live, work, and play together. From the early philosophers and founding fathers to modern practitioners, Dr. Pool-Funai details the need for ethics, virtue, justice, and protection of society's common good. Technological advances, increasing the complexity of society, underscores the importance of both the art and science of good public administration to ensure the government's power to tax, and therefore control, is moderated by appropriate checks and balances. Ethical fiscal policy and adminis-tration becomes the ultimate valve through which 'we the people' can better our lives by guiding those we elect to govern."

– **Marvin L. Dodge**, *Southern Utah University, USA*

ETHICS IN FISCAL ADMINISTRATION

An Introduction

Angela Pool-Funai

Routledge
Taylor & Francis Group

NEW YORK AND LONDON

First published 2018
by Routledge
711 Third Avenue, New York, NY 10017

and by Routledge
2 Park Square, Milton Park, Abingdon, Oxon OX14 4RN

Routledge is an imprint of the Taylor & Francis Group, an informa business

Library of Congress Cataloging in Publication Data
Names: Pool-Funai, Angela E., author.
Title: Ethics in fiscal administration : an introduction / Angela Pool-Funai.
Description: New York, NY : Routledge, 2018. | Includes bibliographical references and index.
Identifiers: LCCN 2017055523 | ISBN 9781138630703 (hbk : alk. paper) | ISBN 9781138630710 (pbk : alk. paper) | ISBN 9781315209258 (ebk)
Subjects: LCSH: Finance, Public--Moral and ethical aspects.
Classification: LCC HJ141 .P66 2018 | DDC 172/.2--dc23
LC record available at https://lccn.loc.gov/2017055523

ISBN: 978-1-138-63070-3 (hbk)
ISBN: 978-1-138-63071-0 (pbk)
ISBN: 978-1-315-20925-8 (ebk)

Typeset in Bembo
by Taylor & Francis Books

This work is lovingly dedicated to my parents, for your careers in public service and unflagging support of my aspirations.

CONTENTS

FIGURES

TABLES

ABOUT THE AUTHOR

Dr. Angela Pool-Funai is an Assistant Professor of Political Science and Public Administration, Director of the Master of Public Administration (MPA) program, and interim Associate Dean of the College of Humanities and Social Sciences at Southern Utah University. She holds degrees from Valdosta State University, Baylor University, and Stephen F. Austin State University. Her research interests include experiential learning, virtual currency, tax policy, and philanthropy. She serves on the Michael O. Leavitt Center for Politics and Public Service board at Southern Utah University, as well as Faculty Senate. She also enjoys volunteering under the dark skies of southern Utah as a Master Astronomer.

PREFACE

Ethical management of public funds entails more than merely avoiding the types of egregious errors that end up on the news. Public administrators are called upon frequently to use their own discretion in addressing a myriad of budgetary decisions, such as whether an adjustment should benefit the long-term goals of the organization or agency versus the short-term needs (or vice versa). Budget managers may also need to decide whether aspects of the budget should benefit certain constituents over others. There are pros and cons to each perspective, with multiple players vying for a piece of the budget.

Seldom are these decisions black and white, and a key purpose of *Ethics in Fiscal Administration: An Introduction* is to tackle the gray areas. Each chapter includes sample cases for discussion and reflection. With the exception of decisions that break the law, there are no wrong answers, per se, in dealing with the issues found in this book. The goal is to encourage the reader to think critically about the options available and analyze the best course of action for the situation presented.

Ethics in Fiscal Administration: An Introduction addresses a need in the public administration curriculum that is currently lacking – namely, incorporating ethical principles into fiscal administration teaching. Although public administration texts exist that explore ethics in a generic sense (or geared toward a specific concentration, such as healthcare administration), this book seeks to fill a gap in the existing literature by fulfilling NASPAA (Network of Schools of Public Policy, Affairs, and Administration) accreditation goals of integrating ethics throughout the curriculum.

NASPAA describes public service values as "pursuing the public interest with accountability and transparency; serving professionally with competence, efficiency, and objectivity; acting ethically so as to uphold the public trust; and demonstrating respect, equity, and fairness in dealings with citizens and fellow public servants."[1] Furthermore, graduates of public administration programs should be able to "formulate judgments with incomplete information, including reflection upon social and ethical responsibilities linked to the application of their knowledge and judgments."[2]

In addition, two expectations for a program holding membership in the NASPAA include:

- Integrates ethics into the curriculum and all aspects of program operation, and expects students and faculty to exhibit the highest ethical standards in their teaching, research, and service.
- Focuses on the preparation of students for *professional* careers in public service, emphasizing both the values and ethics of public service, and the development of professional skills and knowledge.[3]

Ethics in Fiscal Administration: An Introduction guides students to reflect on their ethical responsibilities as budget managers within the fiscal administration curriculum, rather than merely viewing ethics as a stand-alone subject matter.

Notes

1 NASPAA Preconditions for Accreditation Review, 2.
2 NASPAA Standard 5 Matching Operations with the Mission: Student Learning, 8.
3 NASPAA Member Code of Good Practice.

ACKNOWLEDGEMENTS

First, I would like to thank the administration at Southern Utah University, as well as my colleagues within the Department of Political Science and Criminal Justice, for cultivating a work environment that values openness and integrity. Thank you for believing in and supporting our Master of Public Administration program wholeheartedly.

I also owe a debt of gratitude to several individuals for sharing their professional insights as this manuscript developed: Michael Beach, Stacy Bradshaw, Corey Carbonara, Roger Carter, Brad Cook, Rob Dotson, Brant Gary, Gwen Knight, Deena Marchal, Karen Peterson, Ruth Schulenberg, and Mark Stendahl. Thank you, as well, to the anonymous peer reviewers whose valuable feedback greatly enhanced this final draft.

Finally, I would like to thank Rob, Aidan, Jeremy, Donovan, Riley, and Ryan for bearing with me during the late nights, early mornings, and weekends when I needed to work instead of play. Thank you for supporting me through your acts of service, encouraging words, and occasional quiet time to take a nap.

PART I

Government ≠ Business

1

HISTORICAL UNDERPINNINGS OF PUBLIC ADMINISTRATION

In the late 19th century, a scientific feud of epic proportions commenced between Nikola Tesla and Thomas Edison over electrical systems. Patents, bragging rights, and legacies were all on the line as the intellectual battle raged between Tesla's alternating-current (AC) and Edison's direct-current (DC) electrical systems. Even today, any diehard science geek holds an opinion on whether Tesla or Edison was the real Father of Invention. In much the same way, the field of public administration has a complicated and conflicted genealogy.

The "Edison" of the public sphere, to continue with the illustration above, is arguably Woodrow Wilson. Wilson is largely considered to be the father of public administration, primarily as a result of his essay on the topic published in 1887. By contrast, the "Tesla" of public administration is none other than Alexander Hamilton. As a co-author of the *Federalist* papers, Hamilton made a case for the structure and function of public administration, even as the Constitution was under deliberation.

Although the focus of this book is on the ethical utilization of funds in the public sphere, it is important that we delve into the history of public administration first, because the structure of government determines how public budgets will be treated, and forerunners like Hamilton and Wilson espoused different approaches to the bureaucracy. This introductory chapter will cover the history of the American public sector and functions of government.

Development of Public Administration

James Madison, co-author of the *Federalist* papers alongside Alexander Hamilton and John Jay, introduced the term "public administration" in at least two of his own essays. In *Federalist 10*, Madison used the phrase with regard to prevailing distrust of the operation of governments, and in *Federalist 48*, he mentioned the term again in the context of balancing government power through the use of checks and restraints.

Hamilton expounded on the discussion of administration in several of his contributions to the *Federalist* papers. Notably, he shared that he held "... a conviction of the utility and necessity of local administrations for local purposes."[1] In other essays, he commented on the administration of power,[2] the structure of the federal administration,[3] and the powers of administrative taxation.[4] Perhaps even more fitting, given the subject matter of this text, was Hamilton's role as Secretary of the Treasury under George Washington. Hamilton understood the structure of the administration in terms of managing people and processes, and he also had a strong grasp on managing resources necessary to keep the government running efficiently and with checks and balances on power.

Deserved or not, President Woodrow Wilson is widely credited with exerting influence over the development of public administration as a discipline and practice. In his famous 1887 essay, Wilson defined public administration as the implementation of public policy, or "government in action."[5] This landmark paper addressed the discipline and practice of public administration and served as a precursor to formal study of the field.

Wilson purported that geographic isolation, agrarian self-sufficiency, the absence of threats to national security, and limited demands for public services allowed the United States to get by without a need for public service organization or administration. An influx of immigrants seeking respite from government overreach, coupled with the country's buffered geography and largely rural population meant that Americans had little need for social services or enlarged government. In fact, the vast majority of the federal payroll prior to the Civil War were simply postal workers.

Freedom means freedom from servitude to systems too, and popular sovereignty made it harder to organize administration in the newfound land than for a monarchy, such as those present in Europe with which the founders were intimately familiar. Early Americans embraced public opinion, and inviting public scrutiny necessarily makes organizing rule-making more laborious than decisions made behind closed doors. In Europe at the time, a sovereign leader's opinions were only his or her own, and there was no populace to contend with, as far as solicited feedback was concerned. Before the transition to a constitutional government could be fully implemented, however, the citizens of the United States needed to want some kind of change. They looked at familiar models in France and Germany and acknowledged that they were not in search of mirroring political principles that resulted in ecclesiastical oversight and a disenfranchised middle class. One deal-breaker to adopting the European model was the relative absence of self-government at the local level. European local governments were not fully self-government; instead, the bureaucrat served an appointed minister of the monarchy rather than the will of the public.

Federalism and the Complexity of Administration

Federalism is a key aspect to the American political structure, in that authority is divided between the national government and states. Federalism stands in stark contrast to unitary and confederal systems of government. First, imagine a unicyclist pedaling a single-wheel contraption; this individual represents a unitary system, led by a single leader. A totalitarian regime run by a dictator would fall under this model because authority is heavily concentrated and centralized.

Next, picture a bicycle race such as the Tour de France: teams of cyclists ride along the same path toward the same overall goal, but each team is in the race for their own benefit. Every rider wants the prize, and the race is not designed to encourage cooperation between teams. The Articles of Confederation framework adopted by the Continental Congress fits this illustration, since the original states held autonomy for most aspects of government, with little collaboration across state lines.

Lastly, consider a tandem bicycle with two riders pedaling in sync. The person in front navigates the route but relies on the rear rider for assistance powering the bicycle. The person in back contributes muscle and helps balance the bicycle, but must rely on the front rider to guide the way. There exists a give and take – a balance of authority, if you will – between the two tandem riders. This cooperative exchange of power represents a federal system: the national government is the front rider with steering authority, while the states are the rear rider helping to keep the bicycle balanced and moving forward.

Wilson defined public administration as an "eminently practical science," born out of a sense of state. Wilson's milestone essay called for the "running of the Constitution" and encouraged the development of public administration for the Constitution's survival. Wilson responded to concerns about public administration by dividing government into two spheres: 1) Politics – choices regarding what the government should do are determined by majority electorates; and 2) Administration – dictates of the populace should be carried out through efficient procedures, relatively free from political meddling. Most modern scholars reject the possibility of drawing a hard line between politics and administration – as if the two can be completely severed – which became known as the politics-administration dichotomy. This concept will be described in more detail later in this chapter.

Written at a time when government was under scrutiny for corruption, Wilson's essay contended that public administration could be separated from politics. A reform movement was underway to combat rampant cronyism at the state and local levels during the time of Wilson's writing, and since Wilson wanted to expand the capacity of government in terms of its scope and capabilities, he realized the necessity of separating politics from administration in the readers' eyes: "If to keep his office a man must achieve open and honest success, and if at the same time he feels himself entrusted with large freedom of discretion, the greater his power the less likely is he to abuse it, the more is he nerved and sobered and elevated by it."[6]

There is not a single form of government that once appeared simple that is not now complex, argued Wilson. In addition to organizational structure, public administration required some measure of formal accounting. Administrators, Wilson explained, are to implement policies but not have decision-making authority like policy makers. Critics of Wilson's perspective argued that administrators are capable of value judgments that boil down to political choices, yet Wilson asserted that administrators simply discern choices using discretion, which he viewed as distinct from political decision-making. "The field of administration is a field of business. It is removed from the hurry and strife of politics; it at most points stands apart even from the debatable ground of constitutional study."[7] Under Wilson's model, administrative functions involved minor, incremental decisions within the big, policy picture painted by Congress. He rationalized that the former, simple functions of government had given way to complexities.

CASE IN POINT: YOU DECIDE

You are the Chief Financial Officer (CFO) for a state agency. Due to budget constraints, the state legislature has not authorized pay increases for the past two fiscal years. Several department chairs within your agency have voiced concern about not being able to hire quality staff because of the low base salaries offered by the agency. In addition, longstanding pay inequities exist throughout the agency, with certain departments standing out as hot spots, as they lose personnel to parallel moves (but higher-paying positions) in other agencies. The attrition rate within these offices is becoming a serious human resources problem.

As the legislative session concluded recently, you learned that the state has allocated a three percent raise for personnel, and each CFO must decide how to allocate the funds within their own agencies. How do you propose addressing the recruitment and retention needs within your agency in a way that best suits the agency, as a whole, and also boosts employee morale?

Wilson's essay crafted the environment for the bureaucratic development of the United States: "The principles on which to base a science of administration for America must be principles which have democratic policy very much at heart."[8] Administration was not a new concept in Europe, which included several countries with established, complex frameworks of public administration, as noted above. Wilson's concept was popularized in the United States in the early 1900s – an era when the merit system and civil service were in their infancy. Contrary to some opinions at the time, Wilson sought input for his public administration model from overseas, reasoning that the United States could borrow what was good and proven and negate what was not.

Richard J. Stillman demonstrated, in his own essay, how public administration has evolved over more than a century since Wilson's writing. Stillman began his explanation with a statement that the study of public administration necessarily involves an antistatist political outlook.[9] In short, statism is a school of thought that upholds the core organizations within a state, while antistatism is contrary to central government and advocates its limitation. The U.S. Constitution is rife with limitations on government, which serves as evidence of the founders' anti-statist leanings. Even Hamilton, who was an avid proponent of a strong central government, recognized the role of states in thwarting tyranny.[10]

The history of public administration has seen significant changes with each new generation. Author Leonard White, whose first textbook on public administration hit the shelves in 1926, is credited with developing "a logical sequence of steps for practicing 'good' administration"[11] that steered the field for two decades until the Cold War. An acronym for this sequential model is POSDCORB:[12] Planning, Organizing, Staffing, Directing, Coordinating, Reporting and Budgeting (see Figure 1.1). In

FIGURE 1.1 POSDCORB Visualized

Wilsonian fashion, POSDCORB provided a framework for public administrators to conduct the work of government in a methodical, apolitical manner.

In response to the burgeoning civil service and growing interest in scientific and applied research, Robert Dahl's influential text in 1947 infused a scientific, analytical approach into the public administration field. Dahl imbued a scientific perspective into addressing what he considered to be three intermingled problems of values, behavior, and culture.[13] The Reassertion of Democratic Idealism movement – with its politics-forward approach to administration – paralleled the rebellious 1960s and 70s generation in its "cry for relevancy"[14] and fragmented subfields of public administration. The intellectual underpinning of this period of public administration development held that politics were superior to – and separate from – the day-to-day work of the administration.

The end of the Cold War and the call of President Ronald Reagan to rid ourselves of big government prompted the next phase of public administrative thought, known as the Refounding Movement. As with earlier schools of thought, the Refounding Movement was not a single, universally accepted doctrine; rather, several influential clusters gained traction within the movement. Decades later, the definition and practice of public administration remains far from solidified, and each new generation will likely bring even more variant ideas than those that have gone before.

Weberian Bureaucracy

Max Weber, a noted German sociologist, developed the most comprehensive and classical definition of bureaucracy. According to Weber, bureaucracy is the normal way that legal rational authority appears in institutional form; it holds a central role in forming modern societies. For him, bureaucracy was indispensable to maintaining civilization. Weber identified the need for civil societies to accomplish certain tasks, such as building roads, etc., and identified a moneyed economy as an important ingredient. However, his three most important attributes in his concept of bureaucracy were division of labor, hierarchical order, and impersonal rules.

Criticized are his "ideal type" formulations that do not always apply to every society because they may not represent reality. The Weberian model views bureaucracy as highly efficient, but because human beings are not machines, a purely rational approach would be unattainable in the long term. Weber may have sought to "... turn a civil service into a reliable institution of state control ..."[15] by underscoring the formal aspects of bureaucracy (such as specialization, hierarchy, division of labor). However, overemphasis of rigid structure runs the risk of undervaluing the bureaucracy's informal dimensions (including human behavior, relationships, leadership, communication, etc.) in level of importance to performance and efficiency.

Critics of the public sector often note two main problems with bureaucracy: inefficiency and arbitrariness. Inefficiency pertains to administrative systems that operate at less than optimal capacity. Arbitrariness refers to officials acting outside of their jurisdiction, or wielding their authority in a way that offends societal views of justice.

According to Weber, bureaucracy serves as an institutional framework to apply generic rules to specific situations, which ultimately holds government officials accountable to their choices and makes the actions of government just and predictable. Weber contributed much to the understanding of bureaucracy as a social phenomenon. His ideal bureaucracy would legitimately, efficiently, and rationally organize people and work to get things done by the elected leader in a democracy. Bureaucracy, he noted, provides for the role of the individual whose work is interspersed between leader and electorate within a democratic system.

CASE IN POINT: YOU DECIDE

Justice means, first, that the government upholds an obligation to treat people equally on the basis of clear rules known in advance. If Chloe and Caleb are driving their respective vehicles 60 miles per hour in a 30-mile-per-hour zone and a law enforcement officer gives a ticket to Caleb, we might assume that the police also should give a ticket to Chloe. After all, traffic citations can supplement a municipality's revenue, so more tickets issued means more fines collected.

Second, a sense of justice compels the government to take into account the special needs and circumstances of individuals. If Chloe is speeding because she is on her way to the hospital to give birth to a child, while Caleb is speeding just for the thrill of it, then we may share the opinion that the police should ticket Caleb but not Chloe. Justice in the first sense means fairness; in the second it means responsiveness.

Fairness and responsiveness often are in conflict. In the two scenarios mentioned above between Caleb and Chloe, what do you believe is the appropriate response for law enforcement? To what degree should police officers have discretion in such matters? Would you support a "speed trap" set up to catch more drivers breaking the law – however minor – in order to increase fine revenue for the police department?

Wilson argued that the checks and balances inherent in the American constitutional system are reflective of society's desire to reduce subjectivity and clarify official rule. Taking time to be responsive and conduct activities like congressional oversight and judicial review, inviting participation by interest groups, as well as abiding by formal agency procedures necessarily means that the bureaucracy will sacrifice some of the efficiency that Weber held in such high regard. True, constraints such as these may reduce the efficiency of an agency, but also its arbitrariness.

It is difficult for the government to be both fair and responsive if an inordinate number of rules are imposed to impede bureaucratic discretion under the guise of ensuring fairness. Like the example of Chloe and Caleb above, government officials will have less ability to be responsive – taking into account the particular circumstances of special cases – if their primary goal is fairness across the board.

Americans fear bureaucracy's use of discretion to guide decisions and actions, and insist on rules, particularly concerning street-level bureaucracies such as law enforcement agencies, public schools, medical institutions, and prisons. Nationally publicized scandals concerning bureaucratic overreach have only served to solidify some of these fears.

Evolution of American Public Administration

Nicholas Henry[16] described how the field of public administration has evolved and gained ground as a scholarly topic in its own right, particularly as new techniques of public administration are discovered and applied. Considering that most academic public administration programs are still housed within departments of political science, the intellectual and institutional influence of political science on the field of public administration remains prevalent.

Paradigm 1: The Politics-Administration Dichotomy, 1900–1926. Public administration arose out of the need to distinguish between policies of the state and the implementation of such policies. The separation of powers – as evidenced by the legislative (Congress), executive (President and bureaucracy), and judicial (courts system) branches of government in the United States – illustrate the distinction. The public service movement of the early 1900s focused on training for professionally prepared citizens to serve as expert specialists in governmental positions.

Paradigm 2: The Principles of Administration, 1927–mid-1900s. As public administrators became in greater demand for their managerial skills, the focus of the field centered on practical expertise and highly honed skills. The practice of public administration faced backlash as the field progressed toward the mid-20th century, as proponents of scientific analysis went head-to-head with those who sought a more practitioner-oriented approach. Arguments arose as to whether politics and administration could ever be separated or function in unison.

Paradigm 3: Public Administration as Political Science, 1950–1970. Within this phase, governmental bureaucracy was identified as the locus of public administration, but the focus was blurred. There was disagreement concerning whether the focus should be on the mechanics of administration or the philosophical implications. Public administration came to be understood as an arm of political science during this phase.

Paradigm 4: Public Administration as Administrative Science, 1956–1970. This phase roughly coincided with the previous phase, with an emphasis on finding identity within the field of public administration. Organizational theory and social psychology influenced this phase, which also gave rise to the concept of organizational development as it applied to the public sector.

Paradigm 5: Public Administration as Scholarship, 1970-present. The growth of governmental institutes and policy centers has lent credence to public administration in more recent decades, yet there remains a shroud of suspicion among many in academia regarding doctoral programs, in particular, that emphasize practical application over purely theoretical approaches to learning. This shift toward a practitioner focus is evident in competencies identified by the Network of Schools of Public Policy, Affairs, and Administration (NASPAA), which include experiential learning goals.[17]

As public administration has evolved as a discipline, in its own right, so have perspectives on the appropriate role of government. Whether one views the government as an active participant in daily societal life or a hands-off entity that needs to keep its distance will influence how that individual perceives the fiscal responsibilities of the public sector. With this distinction in mind, the next chapter will consider key differences between the public and private sectors.

Notes

1 Hamilton, A. *Federalist 32.*
2 Ibid., *Federalist 27.*
3 Ibid., *Federalist 45.*
4 Ibid., *Federalist 35.*
5 Stillman, R., Ed. (2005). *Public Administration: Concepts and Cases.* Boston: Houghton Mifflin Company, 7.
6 Ibid., 12.
7 Ibid., 10.
8 Ibid., 14.
9 Ibid., 17.
10 *Harvard Law Review.* Defending Federalism: Realizing Publius's Vision. (Dec. 2008). *122*(2): 745–766.
11 Ibid., 20.
12 Gulick, L. (1970). Science, Values, and Public Administration. In *The Administrative Process and Democratic Theory*, Ed. Gawthrop, L. C. Boston: Houghton Mifflin.
13 Dahl, R. (1947). The Science of Public Administration: Three Problems. *Public Administration Review, 7*(1): 1–11.
14 Ibid., 23.
15 Gale, S. A., & Hummel, R. P. (2003). A Debt Unpaid – Reinterpreting Max Weber on Bureaucracy. *Administrative Theory & Praxis, 25*(3): 410.
16 Henry, N. (1975). Paradigms of Public Administration. *Public Administration Review,* 35 (4): 378–386.
17 NASPAA. *Official Standards & Policies.* Retrieved from: accreditation.naspaa.org/ resources/official-standards-policies.

2

THE ROLE OF GOVERNMENT

The first chapter explored the underpinning of federalism in the United States and historical influences on the development of the bureaucracy, as well as the evolution of public administration. This chapter will set the stage for discussing ethics in fiscal administration by drawing a distinction between the public and private sectors.

Profitability and Social Value

In the private sector, a key indicator of success is the value of the business to its owners, be it a sole proprietor or shareholders. Although financial administration in the public sector may share similar managerial tools and technical procedures, governments differ from private businesses in regard to ownership, resource constraints, and overall objectives. Furthermore, governments have the ability to tax, and the value of government services is not always easy to quantify in terms of financial worth.

The goods and services that we use daily come from a myriad of sources, including private businesses, nonprofit organizations, and government agencies. Under market principles of voluntary exchange, we receive goods and services in return for payments made. Public services, on the other hand, are financed differently. Taxes and other revenues accorded by the law pay for services such as the local police department, school district, and road maintenance.

Market Failure and Functions of Government

Concerning the roles of government and business, one might ask: If the private sector has the ability to provide all necessary goods and services, then why not rely solely on free markets? Ideally, a competitive and smoothly functioning market will lead to prices at which buyers' demand matches sellers' supply. The catch lies in James Madison's observation in *The Federalist No. 51*, "If men were angels, no government would be necessary."[1] Reality dictates a role for government, even if private markets could deliver most goods and services. First and foremost, markets need government oversight to function efficiently, enforce contracts, and ward off fraudulent behavior. Second, some services are perceived as the government's responsibility; we refer to these as public goods. Services like police and fire protection, elementary and secondary education, and environmental safety fall into the category of public goods.

Public Goods

Services such as the ones mentioned above may not be available in the private sector, or it would be inefficient to try to offer the service, which leads to two dilemmas regarding public goods: non-exhaustion and non-rivalry. Non-exhaustion pertains to benefits that must be shared; for example, an individual would not have their own fire response team stationed at their personal residence. When public goods are supplied, in this sense, the service benefits additional people without reducing the benefit to the original recipients. In fact, once the service has been provided for one, the cost of adding additional beneficiaries is inherently nominal. (This idea of inconsumable, no-cost benefits is in contrast with the private sector, which charges per good or service and cannot afford to offer sales lower than the efficient price.)

Non-rivalry among public goods relates to the inability to exclude those who have not paid. In the private sector, consumers do not receive goods or services without payment, but certain public goods are available to all. A paramedic responding to a car accident is expected to provide emergency care to the victims, regardless of whether the injured individuals have paid their income taxes or filed for bankruptcy. Furthermore, in some cases, beneficiaries may receive services, whether they want to or not, and there is no opt-out alternative to paying for the service. For instance, a municipal mosquito abatement service may spray an entire neighborhood, without consideration for residents who do not want the treatment, yet they pay for it through local taxes. Insects and wind are no respecters of property lines, so attempting to spray the air at individual residences would be comically inefficient, at best.

Transactions between seller and buyer – or provider and beneficiary – can also affect third parties. These consequences are known as externalities. Some externalities are undesirable, such as air pollution exacerbated by automotive exhaust. Drivers may purchase vehicles based on aesthetic features, horsepower, gas mileage, seating capacity, etc., with little attention given to the exhaust system. Consequently, government tries to offset these market failures caused by externalities by subsidizing low-emission vehicles and/or imposing additional taxes on poorly maintained cars and trucks.

Externalities can also be positive. To help prevent the spread of germs to patients, hospitals nowadays often have complimentary, sanitizing gel dispensers located throughout the facility. People who might not otherwise stop at the restroom to wash their hands before visiting a patient may be inclined to use a squirt of hand sanitizer from a hallway dispenser before entering the patient's room. The sanitizing gel can certainly be of benefit for the individual using the dispensary, but the intended externality is to inhibit that same individual from spreading potential diseases to the patients.

Failure of Competition

Anti-monopolistic legislation in the form of the Sherman Antitrust Act of 1890 was designed to prohibit interstate monopolies. Several states had similar laws on the books prior to Sherman, but they were necessarily limited to intrastate commerce. In the private sector, when monopolies rise to power, they can drive out competition, charge unjustifiably high prices, and position themselves as unopposed in the marketplace. On the public sector side, however, there are natural monopolies, particularly with regard to utilities. There only needs to be one municipal water department, for example. Yet, in cases where private corporations do compete for public contracts (such as electricity and telephone companies), multiple levels of government still regulate entry of new firms, prices charged, and overall operations. Even in such cases, individual electric companies do not erect their own utility poles or build their own substations; they partner with the local government entity for service delivery.

Part of government's regulatory responsibility within a competitive private marketplace is to safeguard against incomplete markets and imperfect information. The laborious process of getting a new prescription drug from concept to consumers, for example, is part of this oversight. Pharmaceutical companies are required to submit updates (and pay fees) to the Food and Drug Administration throughout the clinical trial period. Without such strictly scrutinized testing, as well as requisite disclosures through advertisements and packaging, patients might be uninformed about the risks, alternatives, and contraindications of certain medications.

On the macro level, governments also seek to stabilize the economy by thwarting high unemployment, keeping inflation in check, and bolstering economic growth. Through monetary policy (management of the money supply) and fiscal policy (changes to taxation and spending), government seeks to adjust market failures. The Federal Reserve ("The Fed"), established by the Federal Reserve Act of 1913, was birthed from a general mistrust of the banking industry and serves to oversee financial institutions and manage monetary policy. Its goals are multi-faceted, with an emphasis on creating conditions conducive to full employment and maintaining economic stability. The Fed's toolbox includes the ability to adjust interest rates, purchase securities, and issue currency.

Fiscal policy encompasses the delicate balance between expenditures and enues in the government, or spending and taxation. Generally speaking, taxes fall into two categories: regressive or progressive. Individuals and families on the lower end of the income spectrum feel the pinch of regressive taxes more so than those with higher incomes. Retail sales tax and other across-the-board, or flat, taxes that are assessed without taking income into account fall into this category of regressive policy. Progressive taxes, on the other hand, do not adversely affect lower income earners disproportionately to their higher income peers. Income taxes are the quintessential example of progressive taxes, because those who earn more pay more (deductions, credits, and accounting loopholes notwithstanding).

Redistribution

The private market distributes goods and services of the economy on the basis of supply and demand, but in a purely market economy, individuals with limited resources run the risk of being priced out of participating in the marketplace and may be relegated to a low standard of living. To alleviate economic injustices, governments may seek to protect the very poor by providing programs and services to assist them. The financial system for such services is known as redistribution, because they are paid for with tax dollars – presumably by higher income taxpayers, hence redistributing a portion of their wealth to the poor. Although the United States does utilize some redistributive programs, such as Temporary Aid to Needy Families (TANF), Medicaid, and Medicare, the use of proactive tax and incentive programs is less in America than many other peer nations, particularly in Europe.

Privatization

Privatization entails transferring business operations from government to the private sector. Such transfers could involve government-owned businesses that engage in production of goods and services where competition exists in the private sector, such as waste management. Privatization can also break up the natural monopoly power of certain government-owned businesses, including industries like telecommunications or electricity. On a smaller scale, privatization can involve contracting out publicly financed services to private businesses in the same field, such as bookkeeping or landscaping.

CASE IN POINT: YOU DECIDE

Solely private systems are not fail-safe, either. Consider, for example, private prisons. If a private company is compensated based on the number of inmates housed within the facility, then the motivation to rehabilitate and reduce the inmate population could be overshadowed by the desire to keep as many people incarcerated for as long as possible. When services are moved from the public to the private sector, the measure of success can shift from service to profit. While the case could be made that privatization might save taxpayers money, we must ask ourselves: at what expense?

Proponents of privatization highlight the desire for smaller government that operates efficiently, saves financial resources, and improves the quality of service toward clients or customers. Other benefits potentially include diversifying the workforce with expert personnel, offering greater operating flexibility, and boosting the pace of innovation. However, privatization does not have to operate as either/or (*only* public or private sector); it can function as a both/and cooperative arrangement between the public and private sectors. Several production options come into play, for example:

1. Government provision plus government production. This combination does not involve privatization; on the contrary, the government entity provides the service from start to finish. Neighborhood snow plowing in the winter would fall under this category, when the personnel and equipment are provided by the local municipality.
2. Government provision plus private production. In this scenario, a government entity would negotiate certain services with a private firm, such as contracting with a private cafeteria company to provide meals to inmates at a county jail.
3. Private provision plus government production. In this situation of reverse privatization, a private company contracts with a government agency for services, such as a concert hall paying city police officers overtime for extra security at a large event.
4. Private provision plus private production. This scenario is self-contained within the private sector and does not utilize government entities at all. A privately owned factory that employs its own security guards to patrol the grounds would fall into this category.

What Can We Glean from the Private Sector?

Although the perspective of this text holds that the public sector is, necessarily, different from the for-profit private sector, the two entities do hold some values in common. Cowton, for example, presents three overarching areas of ethical responsibility in business, which we can transfer into the public realm: integrity, responsibility, and affinity.[2]

As Cowton refers to bankers as "guardians of other people's money,"[3] so, too, is the public sector the custodian of taxpayers' money. Integrity is the linchpin for developing a relationship of trust between an individual and the organization in question (be it a banking institution or the government). Cowton goes on to describe the importance of depositors' trust in banks, lest they have no money to lend. The tie-in with the public sector breaks down at this point, because individuals deposit funds voluntarily into a bank, whereas, taxation is compulsory. Nevertheless, public agencies are not exempt from the expectation to treat their clientele with respect and regard to their best interests.

In terms of banking responsibly, lenders must balance risk and return on investment with both shareholders' and stakeholders' interests in mind. In the case of the bureaucracy, however, one might argue that the public is both shareholder *and* stakeholder. The end game of the public sector is not to turn a profit, but still to manage the public's resources reliably. Just as Cowton describes how lending practices should be fair and mitigate potential harm to borrowers, services provided by the public sector should also be conducted in a responsible manner.

Cowton defines affinity in relation to the banking industry as "relationship by choice, a mutual attraction or resemblance,"[4] which refers to the notion of attracting customers by offering financial products that appeal to their personal interests, also known as "relationship banking." In the public sector, certain services are geared toward demographic cross-sections of the community, such as the Women, Infants, and Children (WIC) special supplemental nutrition program. By its nature, WIC serves a particular subset of the population, namely, pregnant women, new mothers, and young children. The agency does not need to draw on affinity characteristics to attract this clientele in competition with other businesses, per se, because the services are specially designed for them already.

Now that we have drawn some distinctions between the public and private sectors, let us turn our attention to competition within each sector.

The Washington Consensus

Under the Fordist paradigm (named after the brainchild of the assembly line, Henry Ford), mass production stems from mass consumption, which begets mass employment. This concept gave rise to middle class jobs in the early-to-mid-20th century, but it has wavered over the past several decades as technology and administrative changes developed. Mass production facilities have given way to specialized niches and increased global competition. The Washington Consensus was an attempt by U.S. lawmakers in the latter part of the 20th century to increase stability, encourage the private market, and establish a more liberal economy.

While efforts to stabilize inflation and foreign exchange rates were a key component of the Washington Consensus, the policy was critiqued for failing to boost flagging international markets, particularly in developing countries. Bekkers, Edelenbos and Steijn noted that in order for a paradigm like the Washington Consensus to succeed, in the long run, it must be able to adapt to an ever-changing international playing field.[5]

The failure of the Washington Consensus to obtain stability hearkens to Kim and Mauborgne's concept of the blue ocean strategy.[6] While their book was written with the business sector in mind, the concept is transferable to the public sector; namely, organizations must harness innovative practices in order to swim beyond the bloody waters of competition and into the clear, where they can stand out from the pack. In the case of the Washington Consensus, if the market is too specialized, then newcomers will have a difficult time breaking through, but if it is too broad, then a bloodbath ensues.

Successful blue ocean businesses make the competition extraneous by identifying untapped market space. In the current era of a knowledge economy – where information itself is a commodity – the public has come to expect answers at their fingertips, which they develop into their own strategic decision-making processes.[7] This steady stream of information spurs competition, and the relevant literature tends to focus on the business sector, primarily.[8] However, the battle for attention is not limited to private business; the public sector is also susceptible to being left in the dust in the information age. In order to keep up with the ever-evolving times, elected officials need to not only recognize the importance of, but also take stock in, innovative ideas in the global economy.

Political opinions span the gamut of the ideological spectrum, and there is no single answer about the appropriate role of government in the U.S. economy. Although we have yet to reach a consensus across party lines, certain historical movements have been integral in developing modern-day American politics, as we know it. The next chapter will explore this linkage between economics and politics, beginning with social contract theory.

Notes

1 Madison, J. *Federalist No. 51.*
2 Cowton, C. J. (October 2002). Integrity, Responsibility and Affinity: Three Aspects of Ethics in Banking. *Business Ethics: A European Review, 11*(4): 393–400.
3 Ibid., 394.
4 Ibid., 397.
5 Bekkers, V., Edelenbos, J., & Steijn, B., Eds. (2011). *Innovation in the Public Sector: Linking Capacity and Leadership* [eBook version]. New York: Palgrave Macmillan.
6 Kim, W. C. & Mauborgne, R. (2005). *Blue Ocean Strategy: How to Create Uncontested Market Space and Make the Competition Irrelevant.* Boston: Harvard Business School Press.
7 Kim, W. C. & Mauborgne, R. (April 1998). Procedural Justice, Strategic Decision Making, and the Knowledge Economy. *Strategic Management Journal, 19*(4): 323–338.
8 Kim & Mauborgne (2005).

3

LINKING ECONOMICS AND POLITICS

If federalism is a tandem bicycle (as discussed in Chapter 1), then social contract theory is the chain that links the gears. This chapter will examine various perspectives of social contract theorists and explore the connection between governing authority and the sovereignty of the people.

Social Contract

In a generic sense, ideologies are: 1) forward-thinking, 2) action-oriented, 3) political, yet, 4) simply stated, and 5) geared toward the masses. This mass appeal builds people's confidence in their ability to affect change through positive action. Furthermore, the fact that ideologies are stated in simplistic terms means that they are applicable to broad swaths of society – unlike philosophy, which is individualized and leans toward the profound and introspective.

Ideology originated in France in the early 19th century and was influenced by widely diverse trains of political thought, such as Antoine Louis Claude Destutt De Tracy (who studied the process of idea formulation, dubbed the "science of ideas"[1]), Karl Marx and Friedrich Engels (who purported that a "science of ideas" was merely a falsehood used for self-justification[2]) and Karl Mannheim (a contemporary of Max Weber who examined the sociology of culture[3]). Because ideologies are political in nature, they are naturally action-oriented. In order to mobilize the masses, one has to appeal to said masses with an action plan. The idea of rallying the masses spans all modern societies, and one important example is social contract theory.

The premise of any contract is that two parties come to an agreement on a particular issue (or set of issues) and concur on a course of action. So it is with social contract theory – the ruler and ruled agree on their respective roles and obligations. Inherent to social contract theory is a presumption of human equality. This notion was a revolutionary conclusion because it led people to challenge the inequality of society's institutions and customs that distribute power and wealth unequally among citizens. Therefore, if people are equal, no one has greater right than another to rule. In other words, the traditional monarchy with its elitist and ceremonial head of state lost relevance in light of this new mindset. Social contract theory represents an act of people exercising sovereignty and creating a legitimate government to which they consent.

Such a collaborative endeavor challenged the strictly monarchical Divine Rights of Kings theory, which assumed limitless power for the almighty monarch. Popular sovereignty goes hand-in-hand with social contract theory, in that power is vested in the people rather than placing the source of all authority with the state. In fact, social contract theory holds that the state is created by a deliberate and rational act of the very people who are subject to it. Social contract theory requires the government to be a legitimate presence in the eyes of the constituents.

The three biggest influences on social contract theory are Hobbes, Locke and Rousseau. Hobbes held to the notion that freedom is only possible when individuals submit to a monarch. In contrast, Locke determined that freedom is greatest when individuals are left alone, unencumbered by a heavy-handed sovereign. Rousseau believed that freedom can be achieved by destroying societal obstacles that oppressed individuals and inciting revolution to achieve equality. While they differed on several nuances, these theorists agreed on three primary facets of social contract theory:

1. Government is not a natural circumstance; rather, as aforementioned, it is an act of the people, and at one time, people lived in a state of nature with no formalized government. Government was deliberately and rationally conceived by human invention. Social contract philosophers wanted to explain why government was created and what was to be its structure and powers. Such a framework depended on how human beings were living in state of nature versus how much third-party regulation they needed.

2. Natural law governs truths that are absolute, universal, and eternal. (Natural law opened doors for later discussions of natural rights and will be discussed in more detail in the next chapter.) Social contract theorists believed that natural law represented a measure by which human conduct should be assessed. Natural law applies to each person equally; therefore, all people are bound by the same code of moral conduct. Consequently, we owe each other certain considerations, also known as, natural rights.

3. To some degree, people are rational and capable of understanding their problems and solving them through reason. Government was created as a rational attempt to solve problems people encountered in the state of nature.

Human nature is critical because it reveals social conditions, social problems and how they might be resolved.

Access to and availability of public goods and services represent two indicators of a just society, but the economic system is often understood as the principal indicator of social justice. As Herbert Simon reiterated, "… public attitudes about the fair allocation of income are necessarily and justifiably a major factor in determining the scope and nature of public organizations in the society."[4]

Hobbes did not fully take into consideration abuses of power by an absolute sovereign or include measures for checks and balances. He pictured the king as not being party to the social contract; therefore, the monarch could not be bound by it. Society and government were distinct elements, thus putting the power of the king above individuals and society at large. (Locke made the same distinction in reverse.) The function of government, in this mindset, was that people serve the government, not the other way around.

While Hobbes believed that a sovereign was necessary, he was forward-thinking enough to realize that not all societies may have one person as their leader. The idea of being able to transfer power to an assembly of individuals set the stage for the idea that bubbled up in the United States that "We the People" hold the power. If legitimate political power comes from people rather than God, then individuals have the ability to become part of the solution. This mindset of popular sovereignty laid the groundwork for separation of church and state.

Locke reiterated the idea that we are all born equal and free; in other words, we are God's property, not subordinates of one another. While, like Hobbes, Locke believed that we have a need for a common superior, he also saw the purpose of such a leader as a protective role – to avoid war and guard property and only bound by consent. To Locke, political power consists of making and executing laws and defending the commonwealth. When an authority figure fails in their duty, the subjects should be able to dissent.

Locke's *Second Treatise* had profound impact on the Glorious Revolution in 1688 (resulting in King James II being dislodged from his throne). Parliament adopted a *Bill of Rights* limiting the power of the monarchy. Among the rights was the power of Parliament to hold free elections, meet frequently, petition the king, and to legislate. It also prohibited the king from suspending an act of Parliament or tax or keeping a standing army in peacetime without legislative approval.

Locke was optimistic about the rationality of human nature; therefore, government restraint was usually unnecessary and even counterproductive. Put in other words, freedom can be found in the absence of restraint. People should be free to exercise their rights as long as they did not interfere with the rights of others. Individual freedom became understood as an essential right and difficult to exaggerate, and individual equality was guaranteed by natural law.

Arguments in favor of private property during this time integrated economics with political theory. This became the foundation for a theory of economic determinism: people's political beliefs and behavior are preconditioned by their economic circumstances. Private property was perceived as essential to people's well-being. Common assumptions of this premise were two-fold: 1) accumulation of private property allowed people to provide for themselves and their families the necessities of life; 2) an individual's property reflected the individual who owned it (a status symbol).

Restrictions on the private property movement included the notion that individuals should not accumulate more than could be used before it spoiled; and, citizens could not exercise their economic rights to the extent that others are denied the same rights. A market economy was seen as the most conducive to individual liberty. Roots of both capitalism and socialism spring from common intellectual soil.

Locke identified three branches of political powers as Legislative, Executive and Federative, with the latter pertaining specifically to national defense. As Dimock implied with regard to Woodrow Wilson, it is easier to categorize the government than to implement it. Administration encompasses not only organizational structure and execution of policies, but it is influenced by politics, as well.[5] In the United States, it is unclear which branch truly has Locke's federative powers: the Executive branch can use its de facto power to engage in defense operations but cannot declare it "war" without the approval of the Legislative branch – which also controls the purse strings, so it is arguably controversial to say which branch ultimately holds federative powers.

Jean-Jacques Rousseau became known as the father of modern radical thought. Rousseau envisioned people in the state of nature as simple, shy, innocent, and avoiding conflict. In other words, life was peaceful but unfulfilled in its natural state. Individuals were innocent but not moral – more animal than human. Rousseau's philosophy was influenced by ancient Greeks, regarding people as human only if they actually participated in affairs of the state. In this mindset, morals can only be developed in an interactive environment. Moral code made human perfection (and even becoming human) possible.

Private property didn't develop until after community, in Rousseau's frame of reference. In order to achieve such a goal, it may become necessary to overthrow the old order and establish a new one under three foundations of moral existence: liberty, equality, and fraternity. Rousseau had an organic view of society, in that each individual contributed to the whole. Society would become a public person, directed by the general will (a combination of all wills of all persons in society engaged in doing what was good for all). The community controls the state and creates moral authority. Property, then, becomes an expression of political power. Property ownership was a social right, not a natural right, to Rousseau. One cannot accumulate unlimited wealth (or unequally), as it could be used to exploit people and become a source of artificial inequity.

CASE IN POINT: YOU DECIDE

A rural community faced unexpected and unprecedented growth, as individuals and families moved away in droves from a nearby metropolitan area into the suburbs, where they could enjoy lower property taxes and larger footprint properties. In response to the growing population, the city council wanted to build a new public park to beautify the community and retain some of its rural, green-space feel. However, the community was landlocked between the metropolitan city and surrounding suburbs, so any growth had to take place within its municipal boundaries. City officials identified the prime location for the park, a five-acre plot owned by a local resident. The city offered a modest sum to purchase the home and land, which the homeowner refused, claiming that the fair market value of the property had increased significantly with the population boom. Using its power of eminent domain, the city eventually condemned the property and took ownership of it, against the homeowner's wishes.

Given what you know about property rights and social contract theory, do you think the city was within its rights to forcibly claim the property when the owner refused to sell? Why or why not? How would you have addressed this situation, if you were a city official?

Rawls' Political Conceptions of Justice

Fairness is at the core of much of John Rawls' philosophy; in fact, Rawls associated justice and fairness hand-in-hand. Rawls' numerous philosophical works concerning social justice hearken back to influence by social contract theorists such as Locke and Rousseau. The oft-touted *original position* raises the question of how and under what circumstances free and equal citizens may cooperate concerning any given situation. The ability to cooperate is like the mortar that holds bricks together and keeps the city walls from crumbling.

Rawls expanded on his principle in a 1989 essay, in which he presented the notion that a cooperative political system entails a certain measure of consensus among its citizenry. This consensus goes hand-in-hand with similar notions of fairness, equity and justice that are important features of social contract theorists. When Rawls outlined his notion of overlapping consensus for political conceptions of justice,[6] the scope of his discussion stretched beyond the realm of politics. While his concern was for the establishment of a just and fair society, the implications of Rawls' model extend further. As a matter of definition, he explained:

A conception is said to be general when it applies to a wide range of subjects (in the limit to all subjects); it is comprehensive when it includes conceptions of what is of value in human life, ideals of personal virtue and character, and the like, that inform much of our nonpolitical conduct (in the limit, our life as a whole).[7]

The four steps that Rawls identified as critical elements of any foundational system of justice form a critical path toward establishing a stable and fair political structure. The pieces fit together as a cohesive unit, ultimately creating a wholly equitable socio-political climate. Deviation from any of the four components detracts from the just nature of the proposed political system. The first consideration in Rawls' political conception of justice is the perception that diversity is permanent. Socio-political pluralism is critical in Rawls' pathway to a just society, because diverse viewpoints concerning religion, philosophy and moral premises form the culture of a democracy. Practically speaking, there would be no sense in seeking consensus if all parties were identical. Varied vantage points lend credence to the process of consensus-building in a democratic society, and fairness implies an equal opportunity.

Secondly, Rawls contended that a single doctrine can only be maintained within a political system through an oppressive exercise of power. Given the aforementioned need for plurality, if one particular religious, philosophical or moral line of thought is desired above others, then the only way to enforce it is to suppress other mindsets. Rawls gave the example of the Inquisition during the Middle Ages as a case in point[8] – in order to promote the Catholic church, heresy had to be kept in check.

Third, any lasting regime must be undergirded by a majority of its citizens. In keeping with his prevailing ideas of cooperation coupled with plurality, Rawls referred to politically active citizens coming to an agreement upon an appropriate path for society to take. The scenario painted by Rawls was one that embraced diverse views, but such perspectives eventually fell into sync under an umbrella of consensus for the sake of the society as a whole. To turn a blind eye to the majority opinion would be to negate the importance of plurality in the democratic society; yet, for diverse groups to concur upon a particular regime would reinforce a wholehearted endorsement by the society's citizens, as a representative whole, that would lend to its stability over the long haul.

Socialism in Protest of Capitalism

With its emphasis on improving the human condition by eliminating poverty and private ownership of production while boosting the welfare state, socialism emerged in protest of capitalism and its perceived selfishness (given its focus on private property and individualism). The origins of socialism date to the French Revolution, but the Industrial Revolution gave rise to socialism as an ideology. Over time, two facets of socialism evolved: humanitarian and scientific socialism.

Karl Marx foretold of an epic conflict between the capitalist and proletarian classes – one in which he believed the proletariat would win, paving the way for a utopia free of class structures, national boundaries and poverty. Marx gained credibility because of his intellectual approach. One of his famous works, *The Communist Manifesto*, developed his ideas of scientific socialism. Together with Friedrich Engels, Marx experienced and studied the fragile, reactionary political scenarios in Europe in the mid-1800s, espousing radical political ideas that were feared by the powers that were. While in England in the late 1840s, Marx wrote his pinnacle work, *Das Kapital*. Marx mistakenly believed that the era of capitalism was ending and soon to be replaced by a socialist revolution. On the contrary, a resurgence of capitalism unfolded and spread across modern society. Capitalism did not (and has not yet) brought about its own doom, as Marx predicted.

During the political turmoil in 19th-century Europe, three factors contributed largely to Marx's ideas:

1. the Industrial Revolution widened the gap between rich and poor;
2. Napoleon's defeat reinforced monarchical power across Europe;
3. science did not solve all human problems; rather, people were subject to a pattern of "compulsive toil," simply to survive.

Marx proposed the concept of economic determinism, which claimed the key human motivation to be economic – influencing both what we value and do. When tensions surface between competing phenomena, improvements result (Marx adapted this idea of dialectic materialism from Georg Hegel). The process involves the thesis (status quo), antithesis (new idea) and synthesis (blending of the good in each). According to Marx, a person's intrinsic value is their ability to maintain sustenance; anything above is surplus. Marx opposed capitalism on the premise that capitalists only pay sustenance wages and hoard the surplus for their own gain. Lenin interpreted Marx's ideas to mean that a dictator should rule over the proletariat; however, some scholars believe that Marx's goal was an egalitarian society based on everyone's willingness to work and share their surpluses with the rest of society.

Economics and Politics in Modern Society

As mentioned above, early attempts to separate the bureaucracy from political influence were ineffective; economics and politics are inextricably linked in modern society. Having an understanding of economic models in this context helps to build the foundation for implementing ethical fiscal administration by interpreting how scholars view the role of government in the context of the larger society.

Liberal democratic theory features capitalist principles from the likes of Adam Smith, Hobbes, and David Ricardo, with political theories of Edmund Burke, James Madison, and Thomas Jefferson. Collectively, this group favored free individual commercial activity within a paternalistic political system.

Scottish economist and philosopher Adam Smith penned *The Wealth of Nations* and is broadly considered the father of modern economics – namely, capitalism. Smith rejected mercantilism, the notion that wealth is determined by the amount of gold amassed, rather than productivity. On the contrary, Smith set the stage for the modern-day measure of Gross Domestic Product, which tracks the growth of the economy. With regard to determining the cost of goods, David Ricardo (a contemporary of Adam Smith) supported a labor theory of value, in that the value of a good must necessarily include the labor costs inherent in producing it.

According to Smith, the good of the whole is best served when each person pursues their own self-interest. Smith's perspective was atomistic, with the focus on individuals. (This is in contrast with a socialist perspective of society as collectivist or organic.) Capitalism depends on private enterprise. In contrast with economic models that advocate equity, capitalism is not malfunctioning when it favors the wealthy. Interestingly, the greatest enemy of competition is capitalists. For example, Herbert Spencer's Social Darwinism perspective of "survival of the fittest" does not just apply to evolutionary constructs; this principle applies to capitalism, as well. Within capitalism, the "fittest" become the wealthiest. Notions of equity or attempting to level the playing field through competition are in contrast with individuals attaining their own economic prowess.

Neoclassical liberal democratic theory emphasizes government schemes in environments that are already democratic, with the separation of powers featured in federalist governments. Edmund Burke, for example, held social and political stability as primary goals. In this perspective, good government assures order in society. Any existing institution had value because it was the product of accumulated wisdom of centuries. Human reason is not competent to dramatically improve social and political systems; therefore, we are resistant to change. Goodness, morality, and even civilization itself are only possible when people create a political society.

James Madison was more moderate than Burke. Dubbed the "Father of the Constitution," Madison had a conservative perspective on popular government, with individual liberty as the main goal. Human nature is aggressive and selfish but unchangeable, and government (if left unchecked) could become oppressive and cruel. Mutual negation, therefore, provides both checks and balances. Madison was concerned about factions (i.e., political parties); he viewed them as an attempt to divide and frustrate the majority. Unlike Burke, Madison sought to localize, not nationalize, politics. His expectation was that the United States would be governed by an enlightened and benevolent elected aristocracy that would protect the interests of the people while not necessarily being bound by their will.

Thomas Jefferson owned several works by French historian and Enlightenment-era philosopher Voltaire and echoed his staunch separationist stance on the church and state. Jefferson's famous description of erecting a wall between the two entities illustrated his concern about potentially tyrannical influence of religious leaders.

Within this mindset of the separation of church and state, the free exercise of religion represents a key expression of individual liberty, yet religious extremism poses a potential threat to public security and the sovereignty of the state.[9] Jefferson held ideas that were left of Burke, Madison, Locke, but not Rousseau. He leaned toward Locke's social contract and natural law. He favored revolution to bring about change and viewed people as the most competent guardians of their own liberties.

Democratic socialism features the contemporary liberalism of individuals like Jeremy Bentham, John Stuart Mill, Thomas Hill Green, and John Dewey. This philosophy favored government action to prevent oppression. Democratic socialism was birthed from a collectivist, less individualistic mindset than liberal democratic theory. The key notion here is that individual happiness stems from the whole society's happiness.

Senator Bernie Sanders brought the term democratic socialism to the forefront during his 2016 presidential election campaign. Sanders ran on a platform centered on government intervention in areas such as healthcare and post-secondary education. In actuality, Sanders' personal ideology is arguably more closely related to New Deal democrat President Franklin D. Roosevelt[10] than actual socialism. Journalist Marian Tupy, for instance, referred to Sanders as a social democrat because "… he believes in a highly regulated and heavily taxed private enterprise, but he does not seem to want the state to own banks and make cars."[11]

The late Michael Harrington, a writer and political activist in the 1970s and '80s, perceived democratic socialism as the answer to ethical dilemmas in the modern economy – a "new morality,"[12] as it were. He saw socialism within democratic civil institutions as a newfound source of hope for an otherwise discouraged public. Robert Gorman described Harrington as an activist beyond his own time, stating, "The welfare state had become too socialist to let capitalism work and too capitalist to permit socialism."[13] Gorman also attributed socialism's failure to gain traction in the United States to socialists' inability to find an intermediary step between capitalism and outright socialism. In other words, where is the compromise between the free market and government-owned business?

On a similar note, Jeremy Bentham advocated positivist law: government should take positive steps to maximize the happiness of society. Bentham viewed natural law as a philosophical dead end. In other words, people could agree on was should be considered "right" but not the leaders. Bentham saw a need for grassroots self-reliance, or utilitarianism. His hedonistic calculator to measure the utility (pleasure or happiness) for the greatest number of individuals in society included 14 categories of human pleasure and 12 of pain, according to seven standards of measurement.

Likewise, Thomas Hill Green held to the notion that freedom is not the absence of restraint. Instead, individual freedom comes from one's ability to contribute to the common good. A prominent leftist thinker, Green laid the foundation for the idea of a welfare state and saw issues such as free education and labor laws as integral to a successful government. Unlike Locke's view of government as a passive entity, Green saw the government as having an obligation to take positive steps to increase the individual liberties of its citizens.

John Stuart Mill was a student of Bentham. His priority issues included free education, trade unionism, equal apportionment of legislative seats, and the repeal of certain tariffs. He also advocated for equality of women. According to Mill, people's motive for kindness is their own enlightened self-interest. Likewise, John Dewey believed in the intellect and dignity of the people, as well as the power and wisdom of individual contributions to the collective good. Dewey also supported a right to equality in political and legal treatment and was a proponent of human rights. He held to the pragmatism idea that all knowledge is tentative and conditional.

Modern Perspectives on Economic Justice

A stable democratic society must include fundamental ideas of justice. Without some measure of fair and equitable treatment, a democracy would trend toward revolt. Kapstein, whose work will be discussed further in the next chapter, explained, "It is hardly sensationalist to claim that in the absence of broad-based policies and programs designed to help working people, the political debate in the United States and many other countries will soon turn sour."[14] Few topics have the potential to rankle the masses more than a perception of unfair treatment. Kapstein's economic models will be discussed in more detail here and are summarized in Table 3.1.

Communitarians are frequently deemed "protectionists" because of their interest in preserving norms within a nation-state.[15] As the name suggests, the communitarian model emphasizes concern for domestic issues, or as Kapstein refers to it, "national welfare."[16] Communitarians are less worried about equality of outcomes than about equal opportunities. Patriotism and loyalty to country are highlights of this framework. Proponents of the communitarian mindset often shy away from topics like globalization and income redistribution, because such issues may imply welfare-reducing policies such as lost domestic jobs. Regarding the expansion of globalism, Dani Rodrik noted, "A cornerstone of traditional trade theory is that trade with labor-abundant countries reduces real wages in rich countries – or increases unemployment if wages are artificially fixed."[17]

TABLE 3.1 Cosmopolitan, Communitarian, and Liberal International Models

Economic model	Focus	Objective
Cosmopolitan	Human Kind	Equality of outcome
Communitarian	National citizenry	Equality of opportunity
Liberal International	Nation-states collectively	Comparative advantage

William Cline addressed communitarian concerns when he noted that "…it is terribly important to make sure that the gains from trade are fairly distributed, and that there is a whole array of other equity oriented policies that make it possible to make sure that the efficiency gains from trade are fairly shared."[18] In other words, communitarians are not opposed to trade, as long as the arrangement is advantageous and not a hindrance.

The crux of the cosmopolitan model, on the other hand, is its emphasis on individuals. According to Kapstein, the goal of this mindset is to reduce poverty.[19] A cosmopolitan defines fairness as equality on a utilitarian, worldwide scope. There is little concern for domestic issues within the cosmopolitan framework, because humankind *is* the community. Cosmopolitans view a world without borders. Taken to an extreme, the cosmopolitan mindset may overlap with communism, in some respects, with its determination to bring the global citizenry on par with each other.

Cosmopolitan ideals carry over into real life in terms of migration and labor. Branko Milanovik noted that national borders are becoming less significant as citizens become more globally minded.[20] Milanovik contended that migration is more viable on a virtual scale with the advent of computer networking technology, though there is still a wide gap between the wealthy and poor worldwide. Globally and domestically, Rodrik noted, "Far-sighted companies will tend to their own communities as they globalize … It is so much easier to outsource than to enter a debate on how to revitalize the local economy."[21] Communitarian critics of cosmopolitan policy argue that an overly strong emphasis on international, individual welfare will detract from national strength and domestic jobs. Rodrick went on to explain, "Markets are a social institution, and their continued existence is predicated on the perception that their processes and outcomes are legitimate."[22]

Liberal internationalism, by contrast, defines its perspective as the "political structure of the global economy, its international institutions and regimes, and how these institutions shape economic relations among nation-states."[23] Echoing the liberal international perspective of free trade and open access, Don Tapscott and Anthony D. Williams' concept of Wikinomics emphasizes mass collaboration on an economic scale by supporting open source development with participation by the public.[24] As in Kapstein's liberal international model, Wikinomics allows everyone to come to the table with input in the fashion of a true public-private partnership. Kapstein focuses particularly on the development and collaboration of the society of nation-states, calling "growth and convergence" key objectives in the liberal international theoretical framework.[25]

The impetus of Kapstein's text on economic justice is creating economic justice across the board. To accomplish this, he embraces the concept of comparative advantage – one's most appropriate commodity to produce and sell. Comparative advantage on a national scale could be produce, technology, or even labor. Kapstein's particular emphasis is a "statist" approach of ethical, more so than physical, borders: "Liberal internationalists therefore tend to conceive of economic justice in terms of the mutually advantageous and non-coercive agreements that states reach through the process of multilateral negotiations."[26]

Liberal internationalism says that poor nations should be able to come to the table with wealthy nations, have a voice in negotiating process, and that resource redistribution should operate through free trade. Sovereignty and equality are the overriding principles of international justice in this model. Kapstein explains, "[P]ro-poor foreign aid policies can hardly substitute for higher levels of trade and investment, which are the global economy's most powerful contributors to growth."[27] Kapstein's concern is that the society of nation-states should focus on their individual comparative advantages so that when they come to the table for trade talks, everyone will have a worthwhile and willing voice to contribute.

Liberal internationalists keep in mind the big picture of the international community. Under this model, reforms should be "welfare-enhancing rather than welfare-reducing" and include such arenas as trade, aid, and investment.[28] The whole idea of comparative advantage is to open the market to producers that were not open before, which dovetails with Kapstein's interest in bringing large *and* small players, alike, to the table.

Critics of liberal internationalism argue that comparative advantage for some countries will inevitably result in lost jobs in another nation-state (i.e., outsourcing). While acknowledging that in the short run, at least, there may be some negative ramifications on domestic jobs, Kapstein and other liberal internationalists accept that hit for what they deem long-term, welfare-enhancing policy:

> [I]f our shared concern is with those who are least advantaged, then we must create an economic environment that promotes every state's opportunity to exercise its comparative advantage and enter the global economy. In the absence of such an environment, the challenge of poverty reduction will prove all the more intractable.[29]

Policy side effects may include the need for domestic workers to retrain or switch careers, and those who are unable or unwilling to retrain may fall through the cracks.

Social contract theory provided the framework to link economics and politics in the young United States. Philosophers and theorists connected ideas of justice, rights, and the collective good to the scaffolding, and our modern-day structure of federalism was constructed. Likewise, contemporary notions of economic justice have illuminated apparent socio-economic disparities in our global economy and the need to level the playing field. In the following chapter, we will expand upon the aforementioned notion of natural law and consider its influence as the foundation of ethics in the public sector.

Notes

1 Destutt de Tracy, A. L. C. (2011). *A Treatise on Political Economy*. Indianapolis: Liberty Fund.

2 Marx, Karl. 1972. *The Marx-Engels Reader*. New York: Norton.

3 Loader, C. & Kettler, D. (2002). *Karl Mannheim's Sociology as Political Education*. New Brunswick: Transaction Publishers.

4 Simon, H. (December 2000). Public Administration in Today's World of Organizations and Markets. John Gaus Lecture presented at the 2000 Annual Meeting of the American Political Science Association: Washington, D.C.

5 Dimock, M. (1937). The Study of Administration. *The American Political Science Review*, *31*(1): 28–40.

6 Rawls, J. (1989). The Domain of the Political and Overlapping Consensus. *New York University Law Review*, *64*(2): 233–255.

7 Ibid., 240.

8 Rawls, J. (1989). The Domain of the Political and Overlapping Consensus. *New York University Law Review*, *64*(2): 233–255.

9 Visconsi, E. (2006). The First Amendment and the Poetics of Church and State. *Raritan*, *26*(2): 114–136.

10 Elliot, O. (March 4, 2016). What Does Sanders Mean by "Democratic Socialism"? *The Hill*. Retrieved from: thehill.com/blogs/congress-blog/presidential-campaign/271652-what-does-sanders-mean-by-democratic-socialism.

11 Tupy, M. (March 1, 2016). Bernie is Not a Socialist and America is Not Capitalist. *The Atlantic*. Retrieved from: www.theatlantic.com/international/archive/2016/03/bernie-sanders-democratic-socialism/471630/.

12 Gorman, R. A. (2004). Michael Harrington's Proposals for Democratic Socialism in the United States. *Soundings: An Interdisciplinary Journal*, *87*(3/4): 455–479.

13 Ibid., 463.

14 Kapstein, E. B. (1996). Workers and the World Economy. *Foreign Affairs*, *75*(3): 16–37, 17.

15 Kapstein, E. B. (2006). *Economic Justice in an Unfair World: Toward a Level Playing Field*. Princeton: Princeton University Press.

16 Ibid.

17 Rodrik, D. (1997). *Has Globalization Gone Too Far?* Washington, DC: Institute for International Economics, 12.

18 Cline, W. (October 2002). Finding Common Ground in Trade Policy. Paper presented to the Center for Global Development and Institute for International Economics, Session 2: Sharing the Gains of Globalization. Retrieved from www.cgdev.org/doc/commentary/Cline_10232002.pdf.

19 Kapstein (2006).

20 Milanovik, B. (2000). *True World Income Distribution, 1988 and 1993: First Calculation Based on Household Surveys Alone*. Manuscript, World Bank, Development Research Group. Cited in Kapstein, 2006.

21 Rodrik (1997), 70.

22 Ibid., 71.

23 Kapstein (2006), 3.

24 Tapscott, D. & Williams, A. D. (2006). *Wikinomics: How Mass Collaboration Changes Everything*. New York: Portfolio/Penguin Press.

25 Kapstein (2006), 7.

26 Ibid., 17.

27 Ibid., 184.

28 Ibid., 185.

29 Ibid., 194.

PART II

Forming an Ethical Foundation

4

DEVELOPING ADMINISTRATIVE ETHICS

In order to understand how administrative ethics are developed, we must first form a foundation on which to base our ethical standards. In this chapter, we will explore definitions of ethics and related approaches, such as natural rights, virtue, the common good, and justice.

Ethics, Defined

Ethics distinguishes between polar opposite mindsets, such as good and evil, right and wrong, virtue and depravity, or morality and immorality. However, not all decisions can be easily categorized as black or white; ethics also requires navigating the vast gray area between the two extremes. After all, what is "good"?

A teleological perspective would say that a good end result justifies whatever process was required to get there. Anticipated results drive decision making. Say, for example, that the executive director of a nonprofit organization needs to cut expenditures in order to maintain a balanced budget. A teleological perspective would justify across-the-board pay cuts of employees as a first step, since the end result would equate to cost savings. This consequences-based view focuses more on the destination than the route taken to arrive there. Utilitarianism – or the pursuit of the greatest level of happiness or benefit for the most people – also falls under this outcome-oriented philosophy. Keeping with the example above, a utilitarian manager might rather lay off one individual, instead of cutting pay of all employees in the organization, because the negative impact would be limited to one person, rather than everyone on staff.

By contrast, a deontological viewpoint focuses on the motives and intentions behind choices made. Principles form the basis of a good decision making process. John Rawls (introduced in the preceding chapter) and Immanuel Kant (discussed in more detail later in this chapter) both ascribed to a principles-based, deontological mindset. A deontological approach to the aforementioned example would find the executive director mulling over the organization's budget to identify possible areas of waste or leeway to trim. The process of identifying how and where to cut the budget – or, alternatively, how to increase revenues – is the most important aspect of this perspective.

CASE IN POINT: YOU DECIDE

James Svara introduced public sector ethics as a perceived oxymoron – a seemingly impossible, almost comical, objective.[1] How have you seen ethical behavior manifested in the public sector? As public administrators, we have our work cut out for us to change this negative mindset about the bureaucracy.

Svara described the ethical dilemma as a triangle of principles, consequences, and virtue (or intuition).[2] Deontologists lean primarily on their principles, whereas teleological administrators would focus on consequences. Our virtue, or intuition, lends a human angle to our decision-making. Based on what you've read so far in this chapter and experienced in your own life, which does your gut say is better: deontological or teleological ethics? Think of an example where you might prefer one approach over the other.

John Adams is attributed with saying, "Because power corrupts, society's demands for moral authority and character increase as the importance of the position increases."[3] For this reason, administrative ethics are paramount. Public sector leaders should have guidelines in place to resolve conflicts of interest and abide by the duties of their office.

Galloping Elephants

Galloping Elephants[4] is a framework of effective public organization concerned with why government agencies perform well, when they do. The elephant serves as an archetypical symbol of a large, cumbersome, lumbering being. Yet, an elephant can run very fast. Pachyderm means thick-skinned, yet elephants display sensitivity in acts of altruism and nurturing behaviors beyond those that are recognized as parental instinct in many animals. Government organizations, or bureaucracies, have a classic status as uncoordinated, oversized, bungling entities, yet many of them perform very well. Called into question for centuries as insensitive, they also commonly display sensitivity and responsiveness to the needs of clients and others.

The "galloping elephants" theorists incorporated existing literature on public organizations to develop some broad hypotheses about what factors are associated with effective public organizations. Rainey and Steinbauer proposed hypotheses about internal aspects of management including employee motivation, task design, use of human resources, and technology. They proposed that factors that influence performance not only include environmental factors and client characteristics, but also factors that to varying degrees are under the control of managers: treatments (primary work/core process and technology), structure, and managerial roles and actions. This notion of balancing inherent and external influences brings us to the question: Who determines what is right or good?

CASE IN POINT: YOU DECIDE

Portions of a national forest and neighboring mountain communities were hit with a bark beetle infestation, which resulted in dozens of acres of dead trees. Amenities adjacent to the national forest include a ski resort, several campgrounds, and a lake popular with anglers and boaters. Public lands agencies proposed thinning the mountainside to clear out the debris, since dry wood poses a high risk for potential wildfire. Environmental groups objected, asserting that the dead trees served as vital habitat for wildlife in the area. Conservationists prevailed, and the trees remained.

A few years after the bark beetle debacle, a homeowner on the mountain set a pile of weeds on fire to clear off his property. Unfortunately, high winds caught the small blaze, igniting a wildfire that would eventually consume more than 70,000 acres and burn for longer than a month. Multiple emergency response agencies and dozens of firefighters worked around the clock to try to contain the fire, which destroyed more than a dozen structures and forced the evacuation of more than 1,500 people as it spread. The loss of wildlife that could not escape the blaze was estimated in the tens of thousands.

The estimated cost of the fire topped out around $7 million. Who should be responsible for the bill? How much liability does the homeowner have? What about the environmental groups and public lands agencies who argued over thinning the trees in the first place? Should the state and/or federal government step in, financially? If so, to what extent should the government get involved?

The Golden Rule as Universal and Just

The Golden Rule has long been deemed a benchmark for interpersonal – and, by extension, political – relations. In the quest to find a universal political truth, the Golden Rule seems to fit the bill. One caveat worth noting is that labeling a maxim as *universal* begs for rebuttal. In the case of the Golden Rule, some scholars disagree whether consensus on a fundamental, global ethical statement is even possible.[5] That said, no fewer than ten world religions view some variant of the Golden Rule as a yardstick by which decisions and actions are measured, and it remains an internationally understood directive.[6]

Standard Rendition: Do unto Others as You Would Have Them Do unto You

The standard version of the Golden Rule that children from both secular and devoutly religious homes can recite from grade school and Sunday School hearkens back to the New Testament.[7] The call to "do to others what you would have them do to you" transcends purely spiritual interpretations and is reiterated as a cross-cultural ethical mandate.

In biblical references, the Golden Rule directive is nestled within a more comprehensive passage about relating to others. The reference in Luke 6:31 pertains to dealing with those perceived as enemies; in other words, even a rival's best interests should be taken into consideration if there is any hope of reconciling the relationship. Empathizing with one's foes is counterintuitive, but it is an important application of the Golden Rule. The passage in Matthew 7:12 expounds on the basic command to treat others as one would wish reciprocated. By adding a universal element to the statement, the Golden Rule finds application not merely in adversarial relationships, but in *every* interaction. The Golden Rule is so highly esteemed that the passage in Matthew described it as summarizing the entire Old Testament Jewish law and admonitions of the prophets.[8]

Inverse Interpretation: Do Not Do unto Others What You Would Not Have Them Do unto You

Saving face in front of one's peers and subordinates is a critical social element in many cultures. At the heart of maintaining honor within one's society and family lies an irrevocable sense of loyalty; in fact, the Confucian perspective of the Golden Rule links loyalty and community as a matter of moral, interpersonal relations.[9] The inverse interpretation of the Golden Rule can be found in both its Western and Eastern iterations and is exemplified in the practice of saving face. To not do something to another person that one would not wish to have reciprocated is akin to not embarrassing the family with immoral behavior or not putting a leader's reputation at stake by pointing out their weaknesses in public.

Economic Axiom: He Who Has the Gold Rules

In addition to the standard and inverse renditions of the Golden Rule, tangential interpretations contort the meaning further. For example, the Golden Rule – where *rule* means headship rather than statute – could be defined as the aristocratic reign of the wealthy, such as the hereditary rule of rich monarchies or the outlandish campaign spending by candidates in a modern, democratic election. Elitism falls into this category, as well, including the cliché that political change does not occur until the wealthy are inconvenienced.

Preemptive Justification: Do unto Others before They Can Do unto You

Although the preemptive justification could be interpreted as aggressive – such as a preemptive military strike in modern warfare – it also has a preparedness angle. For example, a state river authority that performs critical maintenance on a dam before the rainy season is preemptively mitigating a potential disaster before it happens.

Comparisons to Immanuel Kant's Categorical Imperative

As mentioned above, the biblical interpretation of the Golden Rule suggests that the axiom encapsulates not only the Old Testament law, but also the teachings of the prophets. The law, as itemized in the Old Testament, coincides with Immanuel Kant's expression of individuals' rights. Even in modern-day language, it is understood that rights are enforced by laws. Similarly, Kant's notion of virtue meshes with the teachings of the Old Testament prophets, who were said to offer principles of virtuous behavior and vocalize God's decrees. The Israelites were under duty to obey the prophets as conduits of God's instructions.

First Formulation – Perfect and Imperfect Duties and Similarities to the Golden Rule

While his model does not use identical verbiage, Kant's first formulation of his categorical imperative is closely associated with the Golden Rule. The first formulation suggests that one's actions should mirror universal law. That said, such actions ought to be replicable as an example for others to model. This duplicating factor is what likens the first formulation to the Golden Rule.[10]

Kant's categorical imperative refers to the perfect and imperfect duties, which obligate mankind and drive one's actions. One must find a balance between rights and duty and between self and others. Kant explained this ideal balance thus: "It is a human being's duty to *strive* for this perfection, but not to *reach* it (in this life), and his compliance with this duty can, accordingly, consist only in continual progress."[11] He explained the relationship of rights and duty in chart form in his text, *The Metaphysics of Morals*.[12] Perfect duties represent obligations that are rights, either to oneself or toward others. Imperfect duties are, on the other hand, "... only *duties of virtue*."[13]

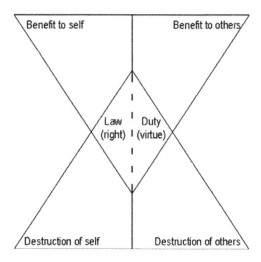

FIGURE 4.1 Kant's Categorical Imperative Reinterpreted

In Figure 4.1, the four-part balance of Kant's original chart (rights of humanity both as individuals and collectively, versus the end of humans as well as humankind) are shown in opposite corners of four triangles. Triangles were selected for this illustration to reiterate the imagery of a fulcrum being the point of balance – in this case, the balance of perfect and imperfect duties. The triangles intersect at the point where law and duty (or right and virtue) merge.

Second Formulation – All Rational Action Stems from Free Will

Moral autonomy is key to Kant's second formulation. The concept of a free will, to Kant, is so innately personal that simply knowing it exists invalidates its function. One's free will must operate according to its own laws. Because the free will answers to no one but itself, all rational action hinges upon it. With regard to interpersonal relationships, the free will has a *perfect* duty to consider both ends and means simultaneously. To treat another person as merely a means to an end is unconscionable, in Kant's view.

Third Formulation – All People Should Consider Themselves Both Means and Ends

According to Kant's third formation, rational beings should act as though they were themselves, both means and ends. While moral autonomy would permit the free will to act outside the constrains of imposed mandates, the self-imposed law governing one's own will must take into account its function as cause *and* effect.

CASE IN POINT: YOU DECIDE

How would you distinguish (if at all) between moral, legal, and ethical behavior? For example, some states may not require motorists to pull over for a funeral procession, but such courtesy is generally seen as moral. From a public administration perspective, what example(s) can you think of regarding activities – particularly financial – that might be legal but unethical? What about examples of morally right decisions that are actually illegal?

Natural Law as a Cornerstone of the American Administrative State

Writing under the shared pseudonym "Publius," then-secretary for foreign affairs John Jay defended the newly proposed United States Constitution by claiming "… that Providence has been pleased to give this one connected country, to one united people …"[14] Such a fervent remark about divine intervention in affairs of the state illustrates a philosophy known as the Law of Nature, or natural law. By examining the historical roots of this viewpoint and identifying key philosophical contributors, this section seeks to analyze the natural law perspective and its application to the modern American administrative state.

Origins of Natural Law

Proponents of natural law believe that a universal moral law coexists alongside physical laws of cause and effect, a philosophy that stems from not only John Jay's Colonial contemporaries, but also scholars dating back to the Greeks. One forerunner of natural law – a scholar who is remembered as a mathematician as well as a philosopher, Plato – explained his ideas in formulaic terms. Just as a perfect circle has no beginning and no end, reason and virtue must be inseparable if they are to function true to form. Although natural law is not a written statute, it entails the notion of a virtuous ideal or a universal reasoning – indeed, the very law of God. For a human law to reflect the law of God, according to natural law practitioners, it must be just, because God is just.[15] This high moral standard of justice is, according to natural law concepts, innate in every human being and unique to mankind. As Budziszewski noted, "We learned long ago that all moral law in the universe is derived from just a few primary moral laws."[16]

If moral law is universal, then it must also pertain to nation-states as well as individual persons. Budziszewski explained, "Moreover, natural law is especially pertinent to *politics* just because it *is* written on the heart, for that makes it a standard for believers and unbelievers alike; not only is it right for all, but at some level it is known to all [emphasis his]."[17] How, then, can evil flourish if – like the

Socratic notion of there being nothing new to learn in the universe[18] – this moral barometer exists in all persons? That which comes naturally must be trumped by choices to the contrary.

Whether attributed to lack of understanding, like Socrates, or lack of reason, like Cicero, later scholars such as Thomas Aquinas and St. Augustine called immoral behavior out for what they believed it was: sin. Porter described that opposition to God's natural law is contrary to the "determinate norms for conduct" that justice requires.[19] The Bible itself indicates that mankind's disobedience is inexcusable:

> For since the creation of the world God's invisible qualities – his eternal power and divine nature – have been clearly seen, being understood from what has been made, so that men are without excuse. For although they knew God, they neither glorified him as God nor gave thanks to him, but their thinking became futile and their foolish hearts were darkened.[20]

Augustine struggled with the paradox of Christians serving as politicians versus the call for Christians to live apart from worldly influences. In *The City of God*, Augustine suggested, "Further, justice is that virtue which gives everyone his due. Where, then, is the justice of man, when he deserts the true God and yields himself to impure demons?"[21]

As did Cicero, Aquinas viewed natural law through the lens of reason, but with a clear focus on God's overriding eternal law. Consequently, an authority figure (preferably a monarchy, to Aquinas) must rule with a balance of understanding between the eternal and natural law. Humans share some inclinations with God's other creatures, Aquinas believed, but certain traits are "good and self-evident" to mankind alone.[22] Logic outside of God's understanding is incomplete, but an elected monarch seemed to Aquinas to be the most adequate structure.

Natural law author Daryl Charles stated, "Because human beings are endowed by 'nature and nature's God,' because it is 'natural' for human beings to act in accordance with their nature as created beings, life has a profoundly sacred cast and therefore must be treated with reverence and a sense of stewardship."[23] If humans are irreparably faulty, sinful creatures, then who is capable of ruling? Augustine answers the query in a sobering job description:

> Given the dangerous futility of worldly ideas, the only aims of a rational politics, other than the maintenance of public order, are to secure an environment free of the grosser sorts of earthly temptations and to facilitate the propagation of the word of God. Those who take responsibility for achieving the aims need to be sober, thoroughly practical people who are free of idealistic fantasy. Politics is a nasty burden that should be borne by dutiful men and women willing to do what is necessary to preserve the pilgrimage, provide security to the pilgrims, and urge them not to tarry along the way.[24]

Implications of Natural Law in the American Administrative State

Robert George noted, "It is a form of practical unreasonableness to reduce ends-in-themselves to mere means."[25] However, understanding the historical context for how and why our Founding Fathers derived the documents that established our country helps us understand where our country is today and guides us in shaping what it will become. After all, asked James Madison, "But what is government itself, but the greatest of all reflections of human nature?"[26]

CASE IN POINT: YOU DECIDE

The beauty of federalism is the amount of autonomy retained by the states to govern at the regional and local levels. Consequently, state laws vary widely, as each state legislature sets its own rules concerning the sale of goods like alcohol and tobacco. The perceived moral implications of these laws cannot be overlooked; after all, the elevated sales tax associated with purchasing alcohol and tobacco is often referred to as a "sin tax."

Such laws can be changed over time and with voter support. For example, among the five states that have historically restricted beer sales to 3.2 percent alcohol by volume, Colorado and Oklahoma legislators have recently acquiesced to change the law. When the changes are put into place, Kansas, Minnesota, and Utah will be left standing as the only states still in a post-prohibition mindset of legislating morality by severely limiting the alcohol content of beer sold in their respective jurisdictions.[27]

What is the appropriate role of government in determining what is good or right for consumers to purchase? Should allegedly immoral or unhealthy goods like alcohol be limited in content without giving consumers a choice? What about taxing such goods at a higher rate? In your educated opinion, do morality-based laws actually change consumer behavior?

Natural Law and Moral Relativism

If natural law is centered on the overarching moral guide of the divine, then the opposite perspective would be moral relativism. Moral relativity stands in contrast to the black and white, right and wrong notions of Augustine, Aquinas and other natural law philosophers. As the cliché goes: "If it feels good to you, do it" – such is the battle cry of moral relativism. By contrast, the precepts of natural law mandate that individual liberty must be tempered by divine law. Finnis put it this way: "But this notion that pleasure, or any other real or imagined internal feeling, is the point of everything is mistaken. It makes nonsense of human history and anthropology. More importantly, it simply mislocates what is really worthwhile."[28]

Virtue

Socrates' contemporaries believed that the body is merely temporal and uninfluenced by the spirit. The immortal mind is key to this doctrine: those who behave badly simply have not yet remembered the soul's past experiences to know how to act virtuously. If this is true, it could be assumed that what a person does matters less than what they think. Virtuous behavior would be an effort in futility, because the body is corrupt by nature. The knowledge of virtue, then, is more important than actually being virtuous.

Cicero went a step further than Socrates by emphasizing that because mankind has the ability to reason, obedience to authority should be a natural result. Unlike Socrates, Cicero believed that knowledge begot action. Because right reason is the cornerstone upon which civilizations are built, obedience to authority applies to everyone, even authority figures – in fact, Cicero might say *especially* those in authority. Cicero advocated a natural aristocracy of deserving leaders, as opposed to nepotism or spoils systems, where preference is given to friends and supporters. Like his Socratic predecessors, Cicero believed that mankind was capable of understanding the right way to behave; the catch was being accountable for putting it into practice.

In a perfect world, a government founded upon reason and a collective understanding of virtue would permit every citizen to pursue his or her goals unobstructed, as Cicero romanticized. Unfortunately, explained Budziszewski, "the common opinion of mankind is not in agreement about what happiness *is* [emphasis his]."[29] Not only does everyone have different interpretations of what makes them happy, but this gives rise to disagreements about what is defined as moral behavior. George elaborated, "Taken together, the basic forms of human good comprise an ideal of integral human fulfillment. To the extent that one's choices are made compatibly with a will toward this idea – as specified by the intermediate moral norms it generates – they may be judged morally upright."[30] As idyllic as it may sound for Cicero and others to set a moral compass based on mankind's collective reason, it became apparent, however, that human nature was more inclined to pursue personal desires over moral understanding. Centuries after Cicero's writings, our Founding Fathers still struggled with infighting among their constituencies, which indicated, yet again, that people tend to be more emotional than reasonable.[31]

Common Good

An undercurrent of the common good is evident in phrases such as "the pursuit of happiness" in the United States Declaration of Independence. Inherent in the authors' perspectives was a sense of community (albeit, not perfect, but arguably better than what they had experienced in the past) and an acknowledgement that stronger powers were at work among them. As *Federalist 12* opines,

This country and this people seem to have been made for each other, and it appears as if it was the design of Providence, that an inheritance so proper and convenient for a band of brethren, united to each other by the strongest ties, should never be split into a number of unsocial, jealous and alien sovereignties.[32]

Put another way, Finnis explained that happiness is not just the wanton search for worldly pleasure; rather, it is a participatory endeavor in the context of community:

But one's self-determination and self-realization is never consummated, never successfully and finally completed. ... So "pursuit" and "realization" are rather misleading in their connotations here, and it is convenient to say that one *participates* in the basic values. ... By participating in them in the way one chooses to, one hopes not only for the pleasure of successfully consummated physical performance and the satisfaction of successfully completed projects, but also for "happiness" in the deeper, less usual sense of that work in which it signifies, roughly, a fullness of life, a certain development as a person, a meaningfulness of one's existence.[33]

Sometimes, happiness for the collective means willing sacrifice for the individual. The founders knew this; in fact, one of the key reasons for writing *The Federalist* essays was to assuage fears of a too-powerful central government. Jay wrote in essay No. 12,

Nothing is more certain than the indispensable necessity of government; and it is equally undeniable, that whenever and however it is instituted, the people must cede to it some of their natural rights, in order to vest it with requisite powers ...[34]

Happiness becomes a vague, evasive ideal, but compromise is necessary to establish (and maintain) order.

Justice

Not everyone agreed that only God-fearing men were worthy leaders. Over time, Niccolò Machiavelli, with his perspectives on empiricism and common sense, stole the spotlight from the natural law movement and laid the groundwork for the enlightenment. The Age of Enlightenment served as a catalyst to mobilize average citizens from being passive toward taking positive action. This new "enlightened" era pushed the belief that people could improve their lot in life by seeking their own solutions to society's ills. This secular epiphany was echoed by scholars and philosophers like Copernicus and Galileo and purported that people no longer had to kowtow to spiritual superiors; rather, they could use human reason to work out their problems. Prior to the Age of Enlightenment, ordinary people did not participate in politics (which were primarily monarchical). Even though elites still called the shots, in most cases, the Age of Enlightenment paved the way for the growth of democracy, which assumes all people are equal and that legitimate authority comes from them, not from the rulers/government entity.

The Age of Enlightenment ushered in a sense of rationalism and activism in addressing societal problems. Science, rather than faith, guided people away from obedience and tradition toward systematic thought. In addition to putting aside spiritualistic thought, traditional skills also made way for new technologies and the urbanization of society.

Machiavelli gave a lot of leeway to government officials concerning just versus unjust behavior. According to Machiavelli's perspective, goodness does not equate with power, and a person in power does not have to be good. The very idea that we would print a book on the topic of ethics and fiscal administration might even make Machiavelli laugh, because from his vantage point, there is no moral premise which to judge a "prince" (or other political leader) for decisions made in office.

Machiavelli scoffed at the idea of gaining knowledge through discovery and cited historical reference only if and when it jibed with his preconceived notions, based on his personal experience. Perhaps his motto was: *If you can't beat them, disprove them!* After all, Alexander Hamilton noted a couple of centuries later, "For, in politics as in religion, it is equally absurd to aim at making proselytes by fire and sword. Heresies in either can rarely be cured by persecution."[35] Hamilton, in fact, had a firm grasp of administration and organizational structure, though other aspects of his writings and political work tend to take prominence over his influence as a foundational voice in the creation of American public administration.[36]

The word *tolerance* implies a sense of moral relativity, an open-armed welcoming of varied viewpoints and ideals. In the spirit of tolerance, no one idea supersedes any other; all playing fields are even. As aforementioned regarding Cicero's rose-tinted theory of reason, the concept of tolerance only works if everyone is in agreement about what they shall tolerate. Charles explains,

> Notwithstanding the arrogance of moral relativists in our day, the ability to make basic moral discrimination is foundational to any just and decent society. To lose this ability is to lose *any and all* basis for a civil order. In the end, "civil society," if we wish to preserve her, reduces to a quite simple – though not simplistic – acknowledgement of baseline moral reality [emphasis his].[37]

Rawls believed strongly that principles of justice ought to guide decision-makers within societal institutions. In Rawls' worldview, social and economic inequalities must be strictly balanced with equality of opportunity, with constant focus on the least advantaged members of society. The concept of public reason is how Rawls sought to improve pluralistic, democratic society. Public reason entails certain norms that are important in the deliberation process, such as basic moral and political values. Public reason boils down to a duty of civility between public officials and citizens. In essence, Rawls believed that democracy should be reciprocal (respecting basic liberties in the exercise of political power) and deliberative (encompassing a broad view of public political culture).

Going forward, the American voting public will have to decide which values it holds in higher esteem: tolerance or moral discrimination. Acknowledging the difficulty in such a choice, Charles noted, "Unquestionably, this will be hard work for American culture at the present time, consumed as we are by 'non-judgmentalism' instead of a resolve to do justly."[38] In the following chapter, we will shift our discussion of moral dilemmas to the role of public administrators as moral agents within the public sphere.

Notes

1 Svara, J. (2007). *The Ethics Primer for Public Administrators in Government and Nonprofit Organizations*. Boston: Jones and Bartlett.
2 Ibid.
3 Adams, J. Attributed.
4 Rainey, H. G. & Steinbauer, P. (1999). Galloping Elephants: Developing Elements of a Theory of Effective Government Organizations. *Journal of Public Administration Research & Theory, 9*(1): 1–32.
5 Burton, B. & Goldsby, M. (2005). The Golden Rule and Business Ethics: An Examination. *Journal of Business Ethics, 56*(4): 371–383.
6 Frank, R. (1954). The Golden Rule – in Ten Religions. *The Clearing House, 28*(5): 276. Wattles, J. (1987). Levels of Meaning in the Golden Rule. *The Journal of Religious Ethics, 15*(1): 106–129. Stanglin, K. D. (2005). The Historical Connection Between the Golden Rule and the Second Greatest Love Command. *The Journal of Religious Ethics, 33*(2): 357–371.
7 Matthew 7:12, Luke 6:31.
8 Matthew 7:12.
9 Wong, Q. J. (1999). The Golden Rule and Interpersonal Care: From a Confucian Perspective. *Philosophy East and West, 49*(4): 415–438.
10 Geiger, I. (2010). What is the Use of the Universal Law Formula of the Categorical Imperative? *British Journal for the History of Philosophy, 18*(2): 271–295.
11 Kant, I. (1996). *The Metaphysics of Morals*. Ed. and Trans. Gregor, M. Cambridge: Cambridge University Press, 196.
12 Ibid., 32.
13 Ibid., 153.
14 Jay, J. *Federalist 12.*
15 Deuteronomy 32:4, Isaiah 30:18, 2 Thessalonians 1:6.
16 Budziszewski, J. (1997). *The Case for Natural Law*. Downers Grove, Illinois: InterVarsity Press, 139.
17 Ibid., 11.
18 Plato (1914). "Meno" in *Plato: With an English Translation*. Trans. Fowler, H. N. New York: G. P. Putnam's Sons.

19 Porter, J. (2005). *Nature as Reason: A Thomistic Theory of the Natural Law.* Grand Rapids: Wm. B. Eerdmans Publishing Co., 6.
20 Romans 1:20–21. New International Version.
21 Augustine, St. (2008). *The City of God.* Peabody, MA: Hendrickson Publishers, 632.
22 Finnis, J. (1980). *Natural Law and Natural Rights.* New York: Oxford University Press, 94.
23 Charles, D. J. (2008). *Retrieving the Natural Law: A Return to Moral First Things.* Grand Rapids: Wm. B. Eerdmans Publishing Co., 5.
24 Portis, E. B. (2008). *Reconstructing the Classics: Political Theory from Plato to Weber.* Washington, DC: CQ Press, 55.
25 George, R. P. (1999). *In Defense of Natural Law.* New York: Oxford University Press, 272.
26 Madison, J. *Federalist 51.*
27 Stephenson, K. (Nov. 9, 2016). Another State Ditching 3.2 Beer, What's in Store for Utah? *The Salt Lake Tribune.* Retrieved from: archive.sltrib.com/article.php?id=4564120&itype=CMSID.
28 Finnis (1980), 95.
29 Budziszewski (1997), 20.
30 George (1999), 272.
31 Ferguson, R. A., Ed. (2006). *The Federalist.* New York: Barnes & Noble Classics.
32 *Federalist 12.*
33 Finnis (1980), 96.
34 *Federalist 12.*
35 *Federalist 47.*
36 Green, R. (2002). Alexander Hamilton: Founder of the American Public Administration. *Administration & Society, 34*(5): 541–562.
37 Charles (2008), 305.
38 Ibid., 304.

5

MORAL AGENTS

This chapter will consider the ethical fiscal administrator as a moral agent and explore responsibilities inherent in such a position. We will also reflect on participation and responsibilities of other parties, including elected officials and the general public. In our modern knowledge economy, there exists a greater demand for transparency and openness on the part of the government, but such expectations also place the onus on the public to educate themselves and bring awareness to potential concerns.

In this context, a moral agent can be defined as someone who possesses the ability to discern between right and wrong and takes responsibility to be held accountable for their own behavior. How, then, does such agency translate into the public sector – and *should* public administrators bear the burden of upholding a moral code for society?

CASE IN POINT: YOU DECIDE

How can public administrators maintain integrity in the wake of the unexpected, or do normal applications of ethical guidelines for allocation of resources in a governmental setting fly out of the window during a disaster? Rapid-fire decisions such as having to choose where to send resources, the order of items, and needs to be addressed, etc. are never easy under pressure.

Federal guidelines such as the National Incident Management System speak to how certain elements should be structured, but some practitioners allege that the directions offer little guidance for making the toughest decisions. In the wake of a natural disaster, for example, suppose you only have enough room at an emergency shelter for 20 more people. How do you decide who gets to stay and who must be turned away? How do you decide where to distribute bottled water and other resources?

Post-incident briefings provide an opportunity to analyze decisions after the fact, but at that point, the examination is untimely and out of context. What suggestions would you have for public administrators facing emergency management budget decisions?

The Public Sphere

Habermas sought to distinguish between the pre-modern era that associated any given ruling entity with God's power and will and the modern (bourgeois) public sphere, which is designed to provide all citizens with access.[1] The public sphere is comprised of literary and political spaces; the former is concerned with issues of the human condition, while the latter relates to general interest concerns.

Because of guaranteed access and the notions of freedom and open communication, state authority equates to public authority. Political participation in Habermas' public sphere is conducted through discourse. The bourgeois public was able to challenge the centralized authority and oversight of nation-states and gained credence as a viable place for deliberation. The liberal model expanded this view that information should be available to the masses.

Given the rise of the welfare state, however, Fraser voiced concerns that Habermas' public sphere failed to take into account new developments of a post-bourgeois society.[2] Her four-part response stated that: 1) social equality is not absolutely necessary for a political democracy; 2) one comprehensive public sphere is preferable to several; 3) public discourse should be limited to issues of common interest; and, 4) civil society and the state ought to be kept separate.

In order to promote generalized understanding, Habermas revised some of his earlier concepts of the public sphere and introduced a normative standard for critical social theory, with the idea of a reasoning public at its core. Communication and rationality contribute to Habermas' notion of modernity and democracy. When free and equal citizens voice their concerns together, it promotes deliberative democracy to help solve societal problems. The public, therefore, becomes part of the decision-making process. Civil society, on the other hand, is comprised of non-governmental/economic relationships of the political public sphere.

CASE IN POINT: YOU DECIDE

Suppose you live in a rural, bedroom community (primarily residential, with very little commercial business). Property taxes have not been raised in 45 years, and the community is very politically conservative. The community prides itself on having one of the lowest property tax rates in the state. Last spring, the city council members met with city staff to discuss budgetary needs for the future fiscal year. Once the proposed expenses were summed, the council had to debate the necessity of raising revenue to maintain the current demands. After arduous discussion, the body decided to pursue the process to raise the property tax revenue. The city council and administration surmised that citizens would want to understand the budget and the perceived need for the increase. Two open house meetings were held at the local elementary school. Very few people attended.

Property owners were sent their initial property tax notices, and people spotted the proposed increase. A group of residents initiated the gathering of signatures to refer the increase to the voters. As this was an election year for two council seats, the opposing group added their spokespersons to the running for those seats. From an administrative and political perspective, chaos ensued. Name-calling, misinformation, anger, and distrust created a toxic environment that led to the loss of loyal employees and elected leaders. A referendum was placed on the ballot and succeeded in stopping the increase in revenue. In the months following the election, approximately $300,000 in expenses were cut, as administration and staff took on more work and services were reduced.

What could the city have done differently or better, in this scenario? Would small, incremental increases over time have been less controversial? What ethical dilemmas did city officials face, in terms of building a viable budget while addressing the demands of the public?

Pragmatism

The gist of pragmatism is that beliefs guide actions and ought to be judged based on their outcomes rather than vague principles. Key pragmatists in American history include Oliver Wendell Holmes Jr, Charles Saunders Peirce, William James, and John Dewey.

Ormerod noted that pragmatism is rooted in classical thought concerning what is real versus what is observable.[3] Just as the scientific method is objective and impersonal, the idea of applying practical standards to other real-world scenarios is an important consideration of public administration. Also, just as scientific experiments must be validated through testing, John Dewey claimed that pragmatism involves a process of reevaluating and revising policies and procedures, as new observations are made.[4]

As public administrators, we must concern ourselves with both the practicality of our decisions (after all, if it isn't justifiable, it will likely be axed from the budget) and the consequences of our actions. This matter of practical, feasible decision-making with an eye on the anticipated consequences falls right in line with the definition of pragmatism. Dewey, for example, noted that actions should be determined based on concrete principles, not abstract ones, because the ends and the means are not separable.[5] Empirical, practical questions should guide the decision-making process.

CASE IN POINT: YOU DECIDE

A hospital's efforts to rein in labor costs resulted in cuts of full-time employees in several departments, including housekeeping. Administrators reasoned that employees could do light cleaning in their respective areas, particularly in non-clinical office spaces, so housekeepers would not have to clean some areas as often. This meant those offices were getting less consistent and thorough cleaning and disinfecting of work areas, which potentially made employees more vulnerable to spreading seasonal infections among coworkers.

Likewise, with the reduction in housekeeping staff, nurses were expected to do more cleaning of their clinical areas, but this meant they were less immediately responsive to patient call buttons and perhaps other clinical work. There was a subsequent decrease in patient satisfaction scores on the "hospital was clean" and "hospital was quiet" metrics, which have direct cost implications by influencing how much the hospital receives in reimbursement. Such feedback also shapes the facility's reputation in the local community.

Picture yourself as a hospital administrator, and you have attended several management meetings in which the most highly paid employees deliberated at length about how to get already overworked nurses to do more cleaning, instead of hiring more housekeepers, who are among the lowest compensated employees. What are some of the ethical financial considerations at play in this scenario, as well as potential unintended consequences that may have been put into motion by cutting housekeeping personnel?

Public Choice Theory

Human behavior also forms the backbone for public choice theory, which is deeply rooted in rationality and neo-classical economics. Public choice theory seems to attempt to address how the consequences of various policy alternatives can be predicted and evaluated. Instead, public choice theory relies on market forces to intervene and prompt action in the economy.[6]

The public choice approach entails the application of economic reasoning to non-market concepts. The notion came about in the early- to mid-1960s as a challenge directed toward traditional public administrative thought. The origins of public administration, often defined by Wilson's classic text, considered hierarchical management to be the optimal organizational structure.[7] Traditional administrative theory involved defining norms as the basis for critical thought on the topic. Herbert Simon and Luther Gulick led the way in challenging the notion that hierarchy was the ultimate model for administration.[8]

Public choice theory has received criticism for being overly simplistic and not adequately addressing the myriad nuances of human behavior. Behavioral economist Dan Ariely described the human condition by saying that:

> ... we are pawns in a game whose forces we largely fail to comprehend. We usually think of ourselves as sitting in the driver's seat, with ultimate control over the decisions we make and the direction our life takes; but, alas, this perception has more to do with our desires – with how we want to view ourselves – than with reality.[9]

In public choice theory, the unit of analysis shifts from aggregated persons to individuals, and public goods are associated with outputs of public agencies. Assumptions about individuals include: 1) people are self-serving; 2) people are rational; 3) people think in terms of maximizing benefits to themselves; and, 4) it is understood that the individuals in question understand all options available to them. Collective action results when people look beyond what is only good to them, as individuals, and collaborate with others.

Rather than seeing overlapping jurisdictions as duplication of effort, public choice theory pictures an integrated hierarchical approach that coordinates more diverse public services within the population than agencies that are entirely independent from one another.

CASE IN POINT: YOU DECIDE

Imagine that you are a city planner for a municipality. The city population is nearly 125,000, while the greater metropolitan statistical area caps at almost 235,000. The city began a pilot, voluntary curbside recycling program in 1998, and by 2011, more than 9,500 households were using the service. The Public Works department estimates that the average household recycles roughly 520 lbs per year, which diverts tons of waste from the city's 237-acre landfill. The landfill's annual report from FY 2011 estimated that the facility has about 12–14 years of life remaining, based on an average of 255,000 tons of waste disposed there annually.

In 2010, the city sought bids to procure services that would create fuel from municipal solid waste. However, only a single proposal was received, and when the city reconsidered the financial costs and benefits of undertaking such a project at that time, they decided to reject the proposal. Since that time, however, interest in renewable fuels has rekindled, so the city has recently posted another Request for Qualifications to establish a Recycling

Waste-to-Energy Project. The city is inviting conventional technology proposals, as well as those that include novel technologies and other waste diversion processes.

Considering the hot-button issue of environmental conservation (on both sides of the political aisle), as well as the short-term and long-term budgetary implications of this proposal, what steps might you take to either encourage or dissuade city officials from pursuing the Recycling Waste-to-Energy Project?

New Public Management

New Public Management (NPM) is based on an entrepreneurial approach by public managers within a political environment that is more business-like than ever before. Budgets are tighter and more public services are privatized. Denhardt and Denhardt popularized the term New Public Service to reinforce the notion that public administrators are servant-leaders who must hold fast to notions of democratic citizenry, community and civil society in their work. Rather than controlling or forcibly guiding society, NPM says that public servants (not to use the term lightly) ought to facilitate an environment where citizens are able to discuss concerns and where the shared interests of the administration and the people are met.[10]

As public choice theory sees the government through the lens of its constituents, NPM adds a layer of values on top of the layer of techniques. In other words, government should not only be run like business in an administrative sense, but also certain business values should guide decision makers. As a normative model, NPM deviates from several basic points that constituted "old" public management: neutrality, centralized, top-down, closed system, rational and effective implementation of policy. Gulick's POSDCORB model (see Chapter 1), for example, fit into the old public management system.

Even the term *public servant* is indicative of the NPM model, in the sense that the public interest ought to be the focus – not a side benefit – of public administration. Other emphases include strategic thinking and accountability, coupled with placing a higher value on people as citizens (not merely customers) than on productivity. That isn't to say that efficiency and productivity should be dismissed, but that concern for democratic values should take preeminence.

W. Edwards Deming

While W. Edwards Deming is known largely in the private sector for his work on quality control in jumpstarting Japan's reconstruction after World War II, his model of systems thinking is absolutely relevant to the public sector, as well.[11] In a systems approach, individuals within an agency or organization do not operate in silos. Instead, they are part of interrelated processes that must work together cohesively in order to deliver positive results. Systems thinking is long-term and cyclical; in other words, there is continual opportunity to learn and improve.

CASE IN POINT: YOU DECIDE

Consider a football game, where the quarterback is preparing a passing play. He expects the receiver to be in position, so the team can achieve a first down. Instead, the receiver is blocked by a defensive player, and the quarterback throws an incomplete pass to the empty spot where the receiver was supposed to be. In a systems perspective, the quarterback would have known to adjust the play and go a different route, thinking on his feet for the good of the team. In this perspective, the team is functioning as an organic unit, not just individual numbers on the field running in prescribed patterns.

Let's translate this example to the public sector: picture yourself as the team leader for a call center. The call center staff are hourly employees who work in shifts to manage calls 24/7. Clients phone in throughout the day to inquire about their eligibility for services. You have found that during certain peak times, clients are on hold for an inordinate period of time, waiting for an available service representative. Sometimes they get tired of waiting and hang up, or submit negative feedback about your office on the agency's website.

You have heard rumors that the call center may be outsourced if performance does not improve. Using the systems thinking mindset of the quarterback in the previous illustration, how might you make adjustments to better serve your call center employees, clients, and budget?

Public administrators are called to uphold the public trust, which is a noble endeavor, in and of itself. Leaders in the public sector are held to a high standard of moral and ethical behavior in the eyes of the public. As we explored in Chapter 4, however, individuals approach ethical dilemmas from varied perspectives, and no one approach is necessarily superior to another. In the following chapter, we will examine ethical behavior throughout organizations, involving both internal and external influences.

Notes

1 Habermas, J. (1991). *The Structural Transformation of the Public Sphere: An Inquiry into a Category of Bourgeois Society* (T. Burger & F. Lawrence, Trans.), Cambridge, MA: MIT Press. (Original work published 1962.)
2 Fraser, N. et al. (2014) *Transnationalizing the Public Sphere*. Malden, MA: Polity Press.
3 Ormerod, R. (2006). The History and Ideas of Pragmatism. *The Journal of the Operational Research Society*, 57(8): 892–909. Retrieved from: www.jstor.org/stable/4102403.
4 Ibid.
5 Ibid.

6 Howlett, M. & Ramesh, M. (2009). *Studying Public Policy: Cycles and Policy Subsystems.* (3rd ed.). Oxford University Press.

7 Wilson, W. (June 1887). The Study of Administration. *Political Science Quarterly, 2*(2): 197–222.

8 Simon, H. A. (Winter 1946). The Proverbs of Administration. *Public Administration Review,* 6(1): 53–67. Gulick, L. (1970). Science, Values, and Public Administration. In *The Administrative Process and Democratic Theory,* Ed. Louis C. Gawthrop. Boston: Houghton Mifflin.

9 Ariely, D. (2009). *Predictably Irrational: The Hidden Forces That Shape Our Decisions.* New York: HarperCollins, 243.

10 Denhardt, R. B. & Denhardt, J. V. (2000). The New Public Service: Serving Rather Than Steering. *Public Administration Review, 60*(6): 549–559. Retrieved from: www.jstor.org/stable/977437.

11 Deming, W. E. (1994). *The New Economics: For Industry, Government, Education.* Cambridge, MA: MIT Press.

6

ETHICAL BEHAVIOR IN ORGANIZATIONS

In this chapter, we will not only look at ways in which organizations can foster an ethical environment from the top down, but also options for individual employees to make their concerns known and promote ethical decision making from the bottom up.

External Measures: Stakeholder Input

Strategic planning is one effective way of gauging stakeholder input by including both internal and external feedback. Universities, for example, often draft five-year or ten-year strategic plans to help guide the institution toward its goals. Beginning the process a couple of years before the previous plan expires is an indicator of good project management on the part of university administration. Rather than wait until the current plan lapses and then scramble to put heads together, the university president may charge the provost or other decision-makers with coordinating efforts across campus (and beyond) to solicit input on the next steps of the university well before the deadline.

In the example above, a well-rounded strategic plan might include focus groups comprised of faculty, staff, parents, alumni, community members, and donors from across the country. These feedback sessions may take the form of town hall-style meetings with the president and other university administrators, or even online feedback via the university's website – which can also be valuable as a means to accept anonymous input, as well. At this point, a draft strategic plan should be made available publicly for additional input.

Strategic planning efforts often fail because they are rushed or are written too broadly to be effective. A plan with goals that seem arbitrary and vague will be difficult to implement, much less evaluate. Consequently, it would be difficult to pinpoint whether or not the university was successful in what it set out to accomplish. A beneficial strategic planning process will move smoothly and transparently from idea to implementation.

Iron Triangles

Iron triangles represent a three-pronged alliance between legislators/decision-makers, bureaucrats, and interest groups, under the guise of crafting or maintaining policies that benefit their mutual interests. Hugh Heclo believed that the iron triangle is too simplistic (even dubbing it "disastrously incomplete").[1] The idea of issue-specific queries from constituents to committee members to government agencies and back to constituents – hence, the triangle structure, which may assume that policy making takes one issue at a time with a few stakeholders – has been challenged since the 1960s with numerous interest groups and more scientific/complex issues coming to the forefront.

These various groups pull together according to commonalities/expertise and form what Heclo dubbed *issue networks*.[2] These networks are quite complex, because assorted expertise means no guarantee of a consensus. Issue networks are more expansive than iron triangles, because in addition to legislators, bureaucrats, and interest groups, they also incorporate the influence of scholars and experts, as well as media attention given to various issues, which might influence how policies are treated (see Figure 6.1).

Heclo called the highly specialized, technical experts *technocrats*. Understandably, technocrats can sometimes make things more complicated than necessary in order to maintain power. They need to feel indispensable, and as ideologues they make it difficult to negotiate (an ideologue would focus on a single-issue group). Consequently, that could pose a problem for policy making through intimidation, delays and prolonging of issues. Heclo was critical of technocrats but acknowledged some positive attributes (which he considered a double-edged sword) in that they perform a useful function and expand participation in the political arena. Policy areas where technocrats have made a positive impact include: environment, healthcare, education and civil liberties. Technocrats can also hamper democracy, in Heclo's opinion, because the required specialization can intimidate people out of the process and make coordination impossible, which would stifle the legislative process.

A potential downside to issue networks is the ramification for the "little people" – those without expert representation, because everyone should have a voice in a democracy according to democratic theory. Heclo believed that the concept of equality could be leveraged in democracy, because equity is a major component in democratic theory that compels us to pay attention and talk about the issues.

Issue networks can also be valuable to the nonprofit sector. Developing partnerships can help nonprofits maximize their legislative goals through coalitions. Speaking as president and CEO of a private foundation, Goodwin borrowed terminology from the business world to explain the value of collaboration in the nonprofit arena:

FIGURE 6.1 Issue Networks Visualized

Two words frequently used in the world of commerce and industry describe the benefits of partnering to influence elected officials to support a goal of a not-for-profit or a coalition of not-for-profits, *leverage* and *synergy*. Leverage suggests the ability to magnify the effort expended and the impact made by one group by enlisting effort and drawing on the resources from other sources. Synergy results in a new resource being created or unleashed when two or more assets are combined. Not-for-profits are learning from this experience and finding new ways to reach their own goals by magnifying the impact of their own vital resources.[3]

Top-Down versus Bottom-Up

Richard E. Matland's objective in designing a new implementation model was to develop a framework that could be useful in putting policy into action.[4] Like

Lindblom, Matland was interested in developing a feasible solution. He investigated two major models: top-down and bottom-up, and identified commonalities in the literature to be useable in the new model: conflict and ambiguity.

In the top-down approach, the policy is very specific, policy goals and values are clear and the federal government has the power to implement the policy. The top-down model is authoritative by definition; consequently, non-ambiguous scenarios favor this arrangement. On the other hand, the bottom-up perspective looks at policy from the service delivery vantage point with consideration for the target population. Local organizations (the bottom of the chain of command) take a micro-view of the policy and implement it as they see fit.

CASE IN POINT: YOU DECIDE

Suppose you are working with a think tank on a tropical disease study in a foreign country. The principal researcher on your team has gained information concerning the local health ministry's failure to report unfavorable water safety details to the World Health Organization (WHO) in a timely manner. You suspect that neglecting to provide the information could have far-reaching implications – not the least of which could include an international scandal if/when a high-profile visitor becomes ill. Refusing to comply with WHO requirements could have dire ramifications for tourism, perhaps more so than admitting to the problem, in the first place. Furthermore, your research team risks losing funding if the project goes downhill. What ethical obligations does your team have to safeguard the public's health, despite potential loss of funding?

Part of your job is to draft the Memorandum of Understanding (MOU) between the think tank and the foreign health ministry. You have received suggestions from others on your team regarding future negotiations of the MOU. One recommendation is to include concessions regarding the reporting deadline – such as allowing reports to be scheduled following tourist season, rather than prior to it. The health ministry would be encouraged to actively publicize safe recreational areas where tourists can enjoy water activities without fear of exposure to contaminants. Is this recommendation sufficient? What other suggestions might you offer that would be mutually beneficial to the think tank's research team as well as the foreign health ministry?

Of the four major types of public policy: administrative, political, experimental, and symbolic, he described each based on its high or low level of conflict and ambiguity. For example, nationwide smallpox vaccination was an administrative policy that was low in both conflict and ambiguity – the health concern was evident, and it was commonly accepted that the vaccine was necessary. An example of a political policy with high-conflict/low-ambiguity is abortion. The issue itself is straightforward, yet it is rife with controversy. Both administrative (smallpox) and political (abortion) policy types are top-down because of their low ambiguity.

Community-based policies (or experimental, according to Matland) like the Head Start program have low conflict yet high ambiguity in how each community implements the services.[5] Being a local initiative at heart, Head Start is a bottom-up policy. Like experimental policy, symbolic policy has high ambiguity, yet it also has high conflict. Knowing this, it stands to reason that it, too, would be bottom-up; however, the model breaks down in the symbolic quadrant. To explain, consider congressional non-binding resolutions – such policies are highly controversial and highly ambiguous, yet coming from the legislature, it seems to be top-down in contrast to Matland's model.

The top-down approach to policy implementation leans heavily on the structure of statutes, from the specific language and legal objectives within the legislation to the theoretical framework around which it is formulated. Compliance and skill are essential internally, while external support helps the policy to be enforced. This school of thought relies on strong leadership and obedient follow-through.

One of the criticisms of the top-down approach is its neglect to include steps of the policy process before it reaches the point of implementation.[6] Public input and historic precedence have little sway in such a model. Another criticism of this approach is the singularly goal-oriented perspective, which makes the policy process appear to be simply administrative, rather than a multi-faceted endeavor. There are also concerns that policy framers who double as policy actors may wield too much unchecked power in a top-down model.

Despite valid criticisms of the top-down approach, there are occasions when such a model is relevant to the decision-making process. One such example is military operations. Due to the need for information security, it is not always feasible to seek weigh-in from all facets of society, or even all ranks within the military. There are times when a command-and-follow structure is vital to the success of a mission. The mission likely has specific objectives and meets the criteria for the top-down approach's goal-oriented structure. It is important to note, however, that the policy framing process in this scenario needs to also include knowledgeable policy actors who will actually participate in the implementation of the choice (i.e., military leaders, not simply politicians).

While the bottom-up approach to policy implementation still takes its lead from policy actors, it focuses on the local impact of policy choices.[7] A particular policy may look different as it is implemented at the national, regional and local levels; therefore, the bottom-up approach is concerned with the factors that may strengthen or hinder policies at each of these levels.

One criticism of the bottom-up approach is that it may make it harder to hold decision-makers accountable for their choices because too much leeway is extended to the actual implementers of the policy. Such autonomy at the local level can backfire when various factions differ on how the policy ought to be implemented.

The bottom-up approach does take into consideration the variety of environments within which policies are enacted, and this can be a beneficial structure in the right context. For example, a state education agency may set parameters for certain benchmarks, but individual school districts have some flexibility to put plans in place to meet the goals as they see fit for their communities. Within each school district, principals and teachers may also have input on ways to accomplish the objectives in a more personalized manner. The bottom-up approach places value on this type of varied feedback.

As aforementioned, both the top-down and bottom-up approaches have a purpose in the policy implementation process. Depending on the task at hand, both approaches may be relevant at different phases of the process, creating a synthesis. During the early stages of policy brainstorming, it stands to reason that broad input is valuable in devising the most feasible solution; in such cases, the bottom-up approach would make sense. In other situations where a reasonable solution is already widely recognized, then implementing policy becomes a matter of following through with clear administrative procedures; therefore, a top-down approach would be useful.

Innovation and Sustainability

Innovative governance is challenging because there are no cut-and-dried approaches that have worked within such varied and complex systems, across the board.[8] Ren mentions one particular management style that seeks to empower employees and aims to boost accountability by incorporating effective motivation and setting appropriate goals.[9] This is especially true in the context of innovation because there is a push to try something new and potentially risky, and workers may be averse to change.

Pedersen and Johansen talk about pulling stakeholders into the innovation process, so that they accept and take ownership of the change.[10] This is a critical step that should not be overlooked, because employees who feel like changes are being imposed upon them – as opposed to those who are made to feel that their ideas contributed to the changes in a positive way – will drastically impact the work environment, and perhaps even the success of the innovation. As Ren notes, "The human component is highly governed by perceptions. If a worker feels that he or she has no utility because of poorly defined function, no authority because of perceived lack of control, and/or no criticality because of no recognition for personal accomplishments, then he or she may become weakly or incorrectly integrated with the system."[11]

Such a fractured mindset among the employees responsible for implementing an innovation could sabotage the entire endeavor. Managers must be conscientious of this challenge to accept changes as positive growth steps for the organization, if the innovation is to succeed.

CASE IN POINT: YOU DECIDE

A state government official describes the biggest competing priorities in the state's funding of the public education system as the Weighted Pupil Unit (WPU) – which is per student funding that flows directly to school districts and charter schools – versus funding specific programs. Some legislators are hesitant to fund the WPU because measuring the results is more difficult; whereas, if they fund a particular program, they can collect data that tells them exactly how the program is working. However, major drawbacks to program-based funding are that it undermines innovation, local control, and allows for little flexibility to meet the varying needs of students.

This debate is ongoing, and every legislative session features an attempt to balance where education funding will go. If you served on the governor's education staff, how would you suggest the state should divvy up public school funding?

The mindset of "That's the way we've always done it" is an archaic notion and a recipe for disaster for any organization that wants to remain viable in the 21st century. As Akenroye points out, "Innovation must be part of the organizational culture. It must be both encouraged and rewarded ..."[12] Innovation models have been widely recognized in the private sector for decades, and researchers like Akenroye are beginning to explore how the public sector can apply this out-of-the-box thinking, as well.

Innovation and Sustainability in Health Care

Akenroye defines innovation as "newness in product or service delivery"[13] and relates the practice to the healthcare industry, in particular. Although certain extraordinary or systemic breakthroughs may fall under the categories of *radical* or *transformative* innovations, most of the innovative factors in Akenroye's study of the National Health Service (NHS) seem to fall under the category of *incremental* innovation. One such change was the NHS' reorganization of its corporate structure over time, in order to address the changing needs of constituents. Similar to forces that propel innovation in the private sector, customer (public) needs and demands also influence innovation in the public sector. Likewise, changes in the competition dynamic within the private sector parallelchanges in public financing in government organizations.

Specific to the healthcare industry, however, Akenroye emphasizes the need for sustainability in addition to factors such as social concerns and supply chain requirements.[14] For example, Akenroye cited technological changes as a key improvement in the way patients schedule appointments in the United Kingdom. Domestically, healthcare organizations are under pressure to digitize patient records for ease of retrieval and economic and environmental sustainability, by not using so much paper. Supply chain improvements include purchases such as high-efficiency lighting and modern equipment to improve efficiency. Another incremental innovation that benefits the healthcare system, at large, is the recognition of social responsibility within healthcare organizations to support local businesses through contractual agreements and deliberate opportunities to participate in the procurement process. Such focused efforts undergird the local economy and improve collaboration between the public and private sectors.

Innovation in Higher Education

Texas is one of only four states that schedules biennial legislative sessions. The bicameral legislature convenes in odd-numbered years for up to 140 days, not including 30-day special sessions that may be called by the governor. Consequently, the budgeting process for more than 200 boards, commissions, and departments and 130 state agencies requires extensive planning and forecasting.

Critics of biennial budgets argue that "[s]uch a system violates the once-standard principle of annuality. The argument is that annual budgets allow for careful and frequent supervision of the executive by the legislature and that this approach serves to promote greater responsibility in government."[15] On the flip side, one recognized benefit to working with a biennial budget is the buffer time available to prepare the documentation and plan strategically for future needs. Unfortunately, in times of economic uncertainty, forecasting so far in advance is especially difficult.

For example, in light of the dire economic outlook in the late 2000s, Texas decision-makers made severe budget cuts in the 2010–11 legislative session. As tax revenues picked up, the state economy appeared much better than projected – to the tune of $8.8 billion.[16] Not all news is good news, however. Many state agencies made preemptive cuts to their projected budgets, resulting in numerous layoffs, and affected agencies began asking where the surplus would be invested. Among those organizations were the state's 101 public institutions of higher education, which faced not only personnel cuts but also funding for financial aid and other student programs.

Public post-secondary education in Texas is regulated by a governor-appointed Board of Regents at each institution. Additional oversight for new degree programs, etc., is provided by the Texas Higher Education Coordinating Board (THECB), a panel comprised of nine members appointed by the governor for staggering six-year terms. In 2011, then-Governor Rick Perry gained both praise and notoriety when he declared the need for a $10,000 bachelor's degree in the state of Texas.[17] One of the ways that higher education leaders brainstormed to meet such a lofty goal was by combining – and in some cases, replacing – traditional classrooms with online coursework in a hybrid, or blended, format.

The Texas State Technical College System (TSTC) is the only state-supported technical higher education option in the Lone Star State, and since its inception in 1965 as a technology institute, the school has pushed the cutting edge of technology to help meet the demands of the current and future workforce. TSTC's fiscal year mirrors that of the state: September 1 through August 31. During the era of budget cuts, roughly half of TSTC's overall annual budget came from funds appropriated by the state and held in the Texas State Treasury. In the fiscal year ending August 31, 2012, TSTC reported system-wide operating expenses totaling $151,035,113.[18] Because of the biennial nature of the Texas legislature, budget planning at TSTC also spans two fiscal years. Therefore, the budget for the 2012 example provided above would have been submitted for review in 2010 for the upcoming cycle.

Appropriated funds, also called Education and General (E&G) funds, are designated for instruction, administration, student services, infrastructure and related needs. Appropriated funds are categorized into General Revenue (from the state) and Other Education and General Revenue (from tuition). During the budget cycle in question, 90 percent of TSTC's appropriated funds fell into subcategories of: 1) Administration and Instruction and 2) Infrastructure and Maintenance.[19]

When cuts are made at the state level, the ripple effect on public higher education institutions like TSTC is felt in areas such as personnel raise and hiring freezes, scaled-back student services and deferred maintenance projects. For a school seeking to stay ahead of the curve concerning new technologies and forward-thinking career paths, cuts to the appropriations budget can be severely inhibiting.

The other half of TSTC's budget is derived from local funds, such as agency funds for student groups, goods and services, plant funds, gifts to endowment, and other restricted gift accounts like research projects. Self-supporting activities such as the campus bookstore and student housing fall into this category, as well. These funds are not appropriated by the legislature and are held and managed in TSTC's own accounts. Ideally, an institution of higher education would have enough endowed and restricted funds to support the day-to-day functions of the school, rather than relying on public funding for operational expenses.

While some of the most prestigious institutions in the country have upwards of $1 million in endowment per student, the biggest players are deeply-rooted private universities like Harvard, Princeton, and Yale, or huge public entities such as the University of Texas system.[20] Without deeply loyal alumni who have equally deep pockets, TSTC and its technical school peers around the country are unlikely to ever become primarily supported by endowed funds. Consequently, the institution continues to rely heavily on tuition income and appropriations from the state to keep its doors open.

In its "Texas Higher Education Quick Facts" report concerning the 2010–11 biennium, THECB reported an 11.3 percent increase in General Revenue appropriations to public higher education institutions, as compared to the 2008–09 cycle.[21] The bulk of that $1.3 billion increase went to universities and community colleges, however. For the TSTC system, General Revenue appropriation funding remained stagnant at $0.2 billion for two biennium budget cycles. Faced with uncertainty amid the nationwide economic recession, TSTC did as many other strategic organizations reliant on public funding did at the time, and began to evaluate ways to scale back and focus on the core mission of the institution, at the risk of reducing and/or eliminating some services and functions.

During the 2010–11 biennium, which coincided with the 81st Regular Session of the Texas Legislature, TSTC presented a 5 percent Budget Reduction Plan report itemizing potential declines in General Revenue funds as part of its Automated Budget and Evaluation System of Texas report to the Texas Legislative Board. TSTC's West Texas campus alone, which is comprised of four satellite sites, made plans to absorb its share of the shortages, totaling $1.2 million in lost General Revenue.[22] Four key areas of cutbacks included: in-state travel, hiring freezes, delayed capital expenditures, and canceling the launch of new programs. The last option concerning new programs is an especially important point for the current budget discussion, because TSTC-West Texas at Abilene was deeply involved in the emerging realm of virtual worlds during the time of these budgetary changes, and the institution had already made extraordinary accomplishments involving educational applications within the institution's distance learning program.

Virtual Education at a Glance

Whether the rationale is to test the waters of emerging technologies or to provide educational opportunities for a broader student base at a potentially lower cost, the prevalence of online education has spread dramatically in recent decades.[23] Like traditional classrooms where some courses are solely lecture-based, while others feature interactive components, web-based courses also vary in format. Some such classes are entirely online, while others are hybrid models with face-to-face components, as well. Callaway hit the nail on the head when he noted that there is little uniformity among course design for both online and hybrid courses.[24] As web-based technology becomes more commonplace, institutions and instructors have liberty to design courses that adapt to teaching and learning styles, while meeting curricular requirements of the college.

TSTC made a radical shift in the delivery method of online education in 2008 when it introduced the first accredited certificate program through its West Texas campus that was fully immersed in a virtual world.[25] The following year, the institution dubbed "vTSTC" had the distinction of becoming the first known college in the world to have a student graduate from a program conducted completely within a virtual environment.[26]

The platform that TSTC used for its virtual world curriculum is a web-based program by Linden Labs called Second Life. The synthetic realm of Second Life is a user-developed, virtual construction zone where users create animated representations of themselves (called avatars) to participate in a persistent, real-time digital environment. The term used for activity that takes place within the confines of such synthetic realms is *in-world*. For the purpose of the current discussion, the terms virtual, synthetic and persistent are interchangeable to describe these digital worlds.

Inside the world of Second Life, users have access to shopping and other commerce, educational pursuits, entertainment and artistic venues, creative expression, interpersonal dialogue and idea exchange. The world of Second Life is divided into parcels of virtual land across a grid, similar to geographical boundaries in the tangible world.

At the time, TSTC owned three sim "islands" in-world, where the institution offered a hybrid selection of courses, primarily geared toward its Emergency Medical Service (EMS) certificate program. The sims included classrooms and meeting space for avatars to convene and hold discussions. Certain parcels were blocked to visitors, which allowed only registered students, instructors and guests to enter the designated area. This security measure helped to protect the classroom environment from casual passers-by who might inadvertently interrupt.

Certain buildings within vTSTC were designated to various programs of study, and the facilities were clearly labeled – much like a traditional college campus – to help avatars navigate their way around the island. The site also included a building named Café 101 that featured a freebie store for avatars to pick up educational and household items to enhance their Second Life experience and help them acclimate to the virtual environment. The coffee shop atmosphere at Café 101 encouraged casual gatherings and provided an opportunity to host guest speakers, much like a conference center at a brick-and-mortar campus.

In the early days of TSTC's involvement in Second Life, the institution offered a broader range of virtually structured courses such as photography and digital media. In response to budget cuts, however, vTSTC shifted its curricular offerings significantly. TSTC was ahead of the curve where virtual education is concerned. During a time when synthetic worlds were largely an unknown phenomenon, vTSTC filled a niche in distance education. Decision-makers at TSTC made a forward-thinking plan to invest salary and operational dollars into a new classroom environment early on, and they succeeded. Although TSTC responded to budget cuts by scaling back funding for vTSTC and repurposing designated Virtual Learning personnel to other areas of the school, the institution's groundbreaking presence in Second Life remains a model example of innovation in public higher education.

In the examples above regarding innovation within health care and higher education, communication and collaboration went hand-in-hand. Both entities demonstrated the importance of public-private partnerships in developing financially sound programs. While communication and collaboration are critical to innovative successes, the next chapter will focus on two additional traits necessary for the management of public funds: transparency and accountability.

Notes

1 Heclo, H. (1975). OMB and the Presidency-the Problem of "Neutral Competence." *The Public Interest, 38*: 80–98.
2 Ibid.
3 Goodwin, R. K. (2001). Developing Partnerships for Greater Success. *The Legislative Labyrinth: A Map for Not-for-Profits*. Ed. Walter P. Pidgeon, Jr. New York: Wiley.
4 Matland, R.E. (1995). Synthesizing the Implementation Literature: The Ambiguity-Conflict Model of Policy Implementation. *Journal of Public Administration Research, 5*(2): 145–174.
5 Ibid.
6 Sabatier, P. & Mazmanian, D. (January 1980). The Implementation of Public Policy: A Framework of Analysis. *Policy Studies Journal, 8*(4): 538–560.
7 Hjern, B. (1982). Implementation Research – The Link Gone Missing. *Journal of Public Policy, 2*(3): 301–308.
8 Ren, C. H. (2012). Micro-dynamic Disturbances in the Government Workforce as a Cause of Poor Organizational Performance. *The Innovation Journal: The Public Sector Innovation Journal, 17*(2): Article 4.
9 Ibid., 4.
10 Pedersen, A. R. & Johansen, M. B. (2012). Strategic and Everyday Innovative Narratives: Translating Ideas into Everyday Life in Organizations. *The Innovation Journal: The Public Sector Innovation Journal, 17*(1): Article 2.
11 Ren (2012), 5.
12 Akenroye, T. O. (2012). Factors Influencing Innovation in Healthcare: A Conceptual Synthesis. *The Innovation Journal: The Public Sector Innovation Journal, 17*(2): Article 3, 2.
13 Ibid., 3.
14 Ibid., 7–8.
15 Lee, R. D., Johnson, R. W., & Joyce, P. G. (2012). *Public Budgeting Systems*. Boston: Jones & Bartlett Learning, 66.
16 Grieder, E. (January 8, 2013). Texas Has an Unexpected 8.8 Billion Surplus: Of course, that could reflect poorly on the state's budgeting process. *Texas Monthly*. Retrieved from: www.texasmonthly.com/story/texas-has-unexpected-88-billion-surplus.
17 Haurwitz, R. K. M. (February 11, 2011). Perry's Call for $10,000 Bachelor's Degrees Stumps Educators. *Austin American-Statesman*. Retrieved from: www.statesman.com/news/news/state-regional-govt-politics/perrys-call-for-10000-bachelors-degrees-stumps-edu/nRXWb/.
18 TSTC System. (2012). Budget. Retrieved from: www.tstc.edu/systemoffice/budget.
19 Ibid.
20 U.S. Department of Education, National Center for Education Statistics. (2016). *Digest of Education Statistics, 2015* (NCES 2016-014), Chapter 3. Retrieved from: nces.ed.gov/fastfacts/display.asp?id=73.
21 Texas Higher Education Coordinating Board. (2010). Texas Higher Education Quick Facts. Retrieved from: www.thecb.state.tx.us/.
22 TSTC System (2012).

23 Guri-Rosenblit, S. (June 2005). "Distance Education" and "E-Learning": Not the Same Thing. *Higher Education, 49*(4): 467–493. doi: 10.1007/s10734–004–0040–0.
24 Callaway, S. K. (2012). Innovation in Higher Education: How Public Universities Demonstrate Innovative Course Delivery Options. *The Innovation Journal: The Public Sector Innovation Journal, 17*(2): 1–18, 15.
25 Flores, E. (July 28, 2008). TSTC First to Offer College Certificate and Degree Programs in Virtual World. *PRWEB*. Retrieved from: www.prweb.com/releases/virtual/learning/prweb1144164.htm.
26 Blanks, B. S. (May 18, 2009). TSTC Takes One Small Step for Virtual Worlds, One Giant Leap for Virtual World Education. *PRWEB*. Retrieved from: www.prweb.com/releases/TSTC/virtual_education/prweb2419874.htm.

PART III

Transparency and Accountability

7

TRANSPARENCY THROUGH FINANCIAL MANAGEMENT

This chapter will look at types of public budgets and the accountability measures inherent with each. For example, line-item budgets can be complicated to adjust because funds are parceled out by category; on the other hand, such budgets can also encourage wasteful spending in line-items with a surplus at the end of the fiscal year. Budget managers are faced with difficult choices to manage such funds ethically. We will also focus on existing checks and balances in this chapter, including accounting standards, reporting requirements, and internal and external audits. This chapter will draw readers' attention to professional standards in the nonprofit sector, as well.

The buzzword *transparency* has floated around public administration circles for decades, and the budgeting process is not exempt from the public limelight. As technology evolves, the public demands detailed information at the click of a few keystrokes. Transparency entails more than simply making data available, however; the information also needs to be readily accessible and understandable. Toward this end, the overall design of a public budget can contribute to (or detract from) openness and promote accountability.

Line-item Budgets

The traditional line-item budget is a classic design that has stood the test of time. This format tends to operate on an annual cycle and cash basis (actual funds on hand), with marginal change from year to year. Political economist Aaron Wildavsky[1] combatted some of the criticisms directed toward line-item budgets, saying:

> Over the last century, the traditional annual cash budget has been con-
> demned as mindless, because its lines do not match programs, irrational,

because they deal with inputs instead of outputs, short-sighted, because they cover one year instead of many, fragmented, because as a rule only changes are reviewed, conservative, because these changes tend to be small, and worse. Yet despite these faults, real and alleged, the traditional budget reigns supreme virtually everywhere, in practice if not in theory.

In a line-item budget, each unit within a budget division is allocated a sum of money.

Resources within line-item budgets are divided into categories, and budget managers have little discretion for utilizing the funds as they see fit, except within the limited context of each line-item. Many grant budgets fall into this category, because grants are awarded based on a specific request with necessary resources proposed for each aspect of the project. In order to move funds from Travel to Supplies, for example, the budget manager or grant administrator may have to contact the program officer at the appropriate funding agency for permission to reallocate the resources to a different category and provide a narrative justification for the change, as well as subsequent reports validating that the change was a necessary step in fulfilling the objectives of the grant.

CASE IN POINT: YOU DECIDE

You are the director of a grant-funded program that serves underrepresented middle school and high school students. Most are first-generation students, meaning that neither their parents nor grandparents hold a bachelor's degree. One objective of the grant is to expose these students to college life by providing opportunities for them to attend field trips to visit university campuses. The school year is nearly finished now, and there is no more time to squeeze in another field trip; however, you just heard about a professional development conference in a neighboring state that you would like to attend next month. The Student Travel line-item still contains funds for field trips, but Staff Travel is depleted. In order to move funds between budget categories, you must make the case for the change and convince the program officer at the funding agency to authorize the adjustment. What is your strategy for the request, and how can you justify the change?

Performance Budgeting

Budgets designed with heavy accountability in mind may be crafted using the performance model. This budget structure is based on future plans and prior performance, with the ideal of getting the most service for the resources allocated – the most bang for the buck, so to speak. Budget managers bear a large responsibility to validate expenses and document successes in order to continue to justify the existence of the program or project.

Performance budgeting can illuminate the goals of an organization by providing a context for success measures. Instead of basing future funding on past spending, this model includes accountability measures. Burke, Modarresi, and Serban explained it this way: "By concentrating on performance rather than compliance, managers could effectively combine the goals of accountability and improvement. Managing, measure, and rewarding results thus became the new trinity."[2]

The Association for the Study of Higher Education's *Higher Education Report*[3] noted several unintended consequences of performance-based budgeting, particularly as it relates to institutions of higher education. One glaring drawback of this funding model is the risk of limiting institutional missions. Arbitrarily capping the credit hour limit in certain programs, for example, may preclude students from taking more electives for a well-rounded education. In another case, if a state legislature prioritizes funding allocations based on growth, then colleges and universities may neglect their responsibilities in areas such as retention and graduation rates because of the demand to recruit new students above other priorities.

An offshoot of the performance budget model is the program design, wherein expenditures are determined by activity, rather than discrete line-items within each category. The emphasis in this model is on establishing relevant spending priorities. In the scenario above about transferring funds from Travel to Supplies, for example, the budget manager would have more discretion to adjust the funding categories based on the overall needs of the program. If the program needed more supplies to fulfill a goal, then the budget manager would have leeway to make an executive decision and reallocate the resources. However, the overall program would still be held to performance standards as devised by the funding agency. One noteworthy example of the program budget mindset is sunset provisions, under which programs are established with a designated time frame to make or break their objectives under threat of being defunded if they do not prove their worth by the deadline.

Zero-based Budgeting

Perhaps the most rigorous funding model is zero-based budgeting. Like the performance model, the zero-based format includes strict accountability measures, in the sense that budget managers must demonstrate that the program is worthwhile to continue. The catch with the zero-based strategy, however, is that the budget resets each funding cycle, meaning that the budget manager must start from scratch to justify requested funds. This model is extremely time-consuming, particularly for budgets that reset every fiscal year. Recreating a budget requires a tremendous investment of human resources, and the subsequent funding request must include documentation of how the previous budget not only sufficed for the projected needs, but also succeeded in meeting the objectives of the program or project.

Zero-based budgeting was popularized within the private sector by electronics giant Texas Instruments in the late-1960s, followed by the State of Georgia adopting the practice in the public sphere.[4] This form of budgeting goes hand-in-hand with program evaluation, because managers must juggle the need for new initiatives versus ineffective or obsolete programs and decide whether to increase, reduce, or eliminate funding. One downside to this strategy is the risk of overlooking potentially effective long-term initiatives that take more than a single budget cycle to become financially viable. Such programs could be flagged as inefficient and placed on the chopping block under the zero-based model.

Checks and Balances

At the federal level, the legislative branch holds the executive branch in check by controlling the purse strings because Congress manages appropriations for federal spending. State and local level entities also face budgetary scrutiny between branches of government, as well as public input. On the heels of the Civil Rights Movement, a slew of federal policies came down the pike in the 1960s and '70s with the goal of increasing transparency in government. In particular, the federal Freedom of Information Act (FOIA), passed in 1966; the Federal Advisory Committee Act of 1972; and the Government in the Sunshine Act of 1976 give the public the ability to obtain and inspect a variety of government documents, attend meetings, and investigate concerns.

While the FOIA does not apply at the state or local level, all states have their own versions of open records/open meetings laws that pertain to agencies and departments within their jurisdiction. Among the materials available to the public are government financial documents, which the public has the right to pore over; consequently, public and nonprofit fiscal managers need to be aware of best practices for handling financial data, as well as requirements for their agencies and organizations.

Accounting

Accounting standards can be defined as "authoritative standards for financial accounting and reporting developed through an organized standard-setting process and issued by a recognized standard-setting body."[5] Domestically and abroad, such standards help fiscal administrators within government entities to know how to conduct, measure, and disclose financial activities of their respective agencies. Domestically, the Governmental Accounting Standards Board (GASB) is the go-to resource for accounting and reporting standards in the public sector. The GASB is not an arm of the federal government; rather, it operates as an independent organization whose standards are recognized as authoritative by state and local governments, the American Institute of Certified Public Accountants (AICPA), and related accounting boards. The AICPA oversees professional conduct and ethics for Certified Public Accountants within the United States, as well as issues specific auditing standards for the accounting field.

As we will discuss further in Chapter 15, professional and trade organizations have their own codes of conduct and established best practices that they abide by within their respective fields. Beyond our borders, the International Public Sector Accounting Standards Board (IPSASB) provides additional guidance on accounting standards, with emphasis in regions of the world like Canada, South Africa, Europe, and Japan.

CASE IN POINT: YOU DECIDE

In a little over a decade, a small suburban community grew from a population of about 8,000 to 20,000. The city had never created a formal plan on road maintenance, and with the population boom, almost all of the roads in the city were due for maintenance at about the same time. Road maintenance tends to be much cheaper than road rebuilding (estimated about seven-fold difference), and with proper maintenance, the life of a road is greatly extended.

Given the urgency of the need, the city council was left with few options but to put in place a maintenance plan through increased property taxes, or continue to under-maintain the roads. The council was torn about needing to raise taxes, but a majority of the council felt strongly it would be irresponsible not to make the smaller investment in the roads now rather than the larger investment later.

Do you agree with the city council's decision? On the flip side, how would you make the case to postpone road maintenance, knowing that it might result in larger costs later?

Reporting

The Federal Records Act of 1950 outlines recordkeeping requirements for federal agencies. These requirements dovetail with the aforementioned Sunshine policies; without accurate recordkeeping, retrieving information would be cumbersome, if not impossible. In 2009, President Obama initiated the Open Government Directive, which incorporated a trio of principles: transparency, participation, and collaboration. The goals of the Open Government Directive hinged on developing a culture of openness and accountability, which included making more information available online and taking a proactive approach to improving communication with the public.[6] In an about-face from the Obama administration, President Trump swiftly took the Open Government Directive offline when he took office.

Transparency in the budget process is certainly of high importance, but budgetary decisions are not made in silos. Executive meetings with advisory groups,[7] foreign officials, and a gamut of examples in between could carry budgetary implications, based on decisions made during those sessions. In other words, transparency in the actual budget process is only one piece of the puzzle. Deliberations about what needs to go into the budget happen in a variety of settings within the bureaucracy, and numerous stakeholders vie for prioritization of those items. Therefore, such meetings are typically open to the press, if not the public, at large.

As of this writing, the Trump administration has scaled back transparency efforts severely, including imposing a live coverage ban[8] during White House press conferences. In related instances, the president disallowed certain media outlets from participating in press briefings,[9] and he excluded American press corps from a meeting with top Russian officials where Russian media representatives were included.[10] The future of transparency efforts at the federal level, at least during the Trump administration, may actually be a return to days past with closed doors and media blackouts. However, the tide has turned before, and it can turn again with continued pressure from the public and media. For further discussion of the Open Government Directive, in particular, see *Developing an Ethical Framework* in Chapter 15.

At the federal level, individual offices have responsibility for maintaining certain records. For example, the Office of Personnel Management (OPM) is responsible for archiving employment records used by the agency in official business ranging from hiring and benefits to retirement. In keeping with best practices, financial disclosures for government entities should address the assets and liabilities of the agency, costs of services rendered, and taxes and/or other revenues collected.[11]

Auditing

The Federal Audit Clearinghouse, an arm of the Office of Management and Budget (OMB), works with federal agencies and recipients of federal grant funds to ensure compliance with audit requirements. In addition, the OMB publishes "circulars" to provide instruction on financial accountability, including auditing requirements. Auditing can be conducted internally or externally, with benefits inherent in both practices. Internal auditors come alongside management "… by independently evaluating the adequacy and effectiveness of governance, risk management and control processes."[12] A key advantage of an internal auditor is institutional knowledge, in that the individual should already be familiar with the culture and policies of the organization they are evaluating.

Involving an unbiased third party in the form of an external auditor can also be beneficial. The external auditor likely will not have the type of implicit biases toward the agency or organization that internal constituents would be at risk of having. The external auditor can approach the review methodically and objectively. Scott and Hawke[13] argue that a key benefit of an external audit "… is the motivation it will provide for that institution to document, critique and then enhance its internal capability for continuous quality assurance, improvement and innovation."

Nonprofit organizations are not exempt from fiscal accountability; in fact, grant makers increasingly require charitable organizations to provide audited financial statements as supplemental documentation for grant applications. Depending on the size and scope of the nonprofit organization, and the state in which its headquarters operate, a charitable organization may not be required to conduct routine audits, but external funders (particularly for state or federal grants) may require this additional step to gauge the financial health of the organization before funding is awarded.

Developing a culture of transparency within the public and nonprofit sectors is a critical step, but having built-in accountability measures will not exempt an agency or organization from critique and influence. In the next chapter, we will explore the political influence on the budget-making process.

Notes

1 Wildavsky, A. (1978). A Budget for All Seasons? Why the Traditional Budget Lasts. *Public Administration Review, 38*(6): 501.
2 Burke, J. C., Modarresi, S., & Serban, A. M. (1999). Performance: Shouldn't it Count for Something in State Budgeting? *Change, 31*(6): 16–24.
3 ASHE (2013). *Higher Education Report, 39*(2): 71–77.
4 Carter, W. H. & Meenach, L. (1977). Zero-Base Budgeting and Program Evaluation. *Journal of Rehabilitation, 43*(1): 18–48.
5 Financial Reporting and Assurance Standards – Canada. www.frascanada.ca/public-sector-accounting-board/what-we-do/about-psab/item55777.aspx.
6 Open Government Directive. https://obamawhitehouse.archives.gov/open/docum ents/open-government-directive.
7 Gerstein, J. (February 2, 2017). Trump May Be Skirting Transparency Law on Advisory Boards. *Politico.* Retrieved from: www.politico.com/story/2017/02/trump-transpa rency-law-advisory-boards-234583.
8 Stelter, B. (June 23, 2017). Why Are these White House Briefings Heard but Not Seen? Retrieved from: money.cnn.com/2017/06/22/media/audio-only-white-house-briefing-journalist-objections/index.html.
9 BBC. (February 25, 2017). White House Bans Certain News Media from Briefing. Retrieved from: www.bbc.com/news/world-us-canada-39085235.
10 Davis, J. H. (May 10, 2017). Trump Bars U.S. Press, but Not Russia's, at Meeting with Russian Officials. Retrieved from: www.nytimes.com/2017/05/10/us/politics/trump-russia-meeting-american-reporters-blocked.html.
11 Office of Personnel Management. (2017). Our Agency. Retrieved from: www.opm.gov/about-us.
12 Janse van Rensburg, J. O. & Coetzee, P. (2015). Internal Audit Public Sector Capability: A case study. *Journal of Public Affairs, 6*(2): 181–191.
13 Scott, G. & Hawke, I. (2003). Using an External Quality Audit as a Lever for Institutional Change. *Assessment & Evaluation in Higher Education, 28*(3): 323–332, 330.

8

POLITICAL INFLUENCES ON PUBLIC BUDGETS

In this chapter, we will examine various political theories concerning public budgets. In addition to longstanding perspectives of reformism, incrementalism, determinism, and satisficing, we will incorporate punctuated equilibrium as a contemporary view of the policy making process.

Reformism

The private sector cliché, "It's not personal; it's business," may also apply to reformism, as a construct for public budgeting. Ruhil et al.[1] describe the impetus for reformism as follows: "The history of reform in the United States can be viewed as a continual search for an ideal governmental form that can deliver services in an efficient, accountable, and responsive manner." This budget strategy takes a black-and-white, ideally impartial, approach to necessary changes in the budget. Rather than favoring pet projects or acquiescing to the political winds of the day, the reformism mindset considers the budget on objective grounds.

After all, a heart surgeon will not arbitrarily perform cosmetic surgery on a patient, just because they have a whim to – the doctor focuses on the task at hand. Reformism is much the same, in that the budget revision process is more clinical than subjective. In reality, however, even the appearance of reform can have positive benefits for an elected official – particularly at the local level, as Ruhil et al. describe.[2] Local leaders who advocate for budgetary reform may gain reputational clout, even if the initiative fails.

Incrementalism

The classical view popularized by Charles Lindblom and Robert Dahl, incrementalism, seeks only minor tweaks to the status quo, not sweeping changes.[3]

The imagery of incrementalism is a gently sloping hill, which can be hiked one step at a time. This budgetary approach does not feature steep inclines or drastic changes in elevation. Lindblom points to two reasons why decisions seldom deviate far from the status quo, namely, bargaining and procedures.[4] Negotiation plays an important role in incrementalism, as potential adjustments are discussed and merits of various suggestions are weighed. However, the premise of negotiation is a cooperative give-and-take, not a radical overhaul, so systemic adjustments tend to happen slowly, as stakeholders negotiate priorities. In a similar vein, established policies and procedures for submitting changes often preclude sweeping changes. Consider, for example, how many months in advance of the next fiscal year the budget process begins at your organization.

Charles Lindblom's model of decision-making theory features two strategies: *root* and *branch*. The root strategy is based on the botany concept that examining a tree's roots tells one about the health of the tree as a whole. It addresses preferences, or what Lindblom considers pie in the sky, and is comparable to what is known as the rational-comprehensive model of decision-making. Lindblom sees the major obstacle to the rational-comprehensive model as not favoring compromise; instead its very thorough focus is on "A-Z." The root method takes a means-end approach, in which the desired end results are isolated, and then the means are devised to achieve the goals. Therefore, a good policy from the perspective of the root method is one that identifies the most appropriate means to reach the pre-selected ends.

The root method is thorough and leans heavily on theory. Values must be collaborative and stable in order for the root method to succeed. The notion of "muddling through," or entangled processes, is demonstrated in Lindblom's argument that even if you arrived at the ideal solution, there would still be a problem: political feasibility! In order to get something through Congress, you have to be willing to compromise.

The branch strategy, by contrast, focuses on past considerations and compromise. Like a branch of a tree, the emphasis here is to take a piece of the problem at a time and look at it. Lindblom favors this strategy because it appears feasible – the actual way real decisions are made (rather than a hypothetical example of how decisions can be made). It is the difference between empirical (what *is*) and normative (what *should be*). Lindblom cites the lack of time and resources available to use the root method. The positive reasons for using the branch model are the incremental, or marginal, measured decision-making that takes place. Errors can be fixed more easily while still small and adjust as needed.

The branch, or successive limited comparisons method, chooses means and ends simultaneously. This method does not lend itself well to analysis, and vital potential outcomes and affected values are neglected, because it is impossible to take every important detail into consideration when you are planning steps and goals simultaneously. Unlike the root method, which relies on established theory, the branch method unfolds and folds back over time, creating a chronological, cyclical process for policy making.

CASE IN POINT: YOU DECIDE

Employees at a state agency had been promised a raise by the agency's directors for several years. Each director lobbied the state legislature for an increase in budgetary funds to provide this raise, but were generally unsuccessful. Sometimes a revised lower budget was approved that resulted in very small raises, but nothing like what had been promised. The primary concern was that these professionals were not receiving the same salaries as their counterparts at another state agency. Because of the nature of their work, the staff all were required to have advanced degrees and special licensing. The directors' arguments to the legislature always included the fact that it was difficult to retain these highly trained professionals because of the low salary and the lack of parity with other professionals doing similar work.

Several of these employees were passionate about their jobs and had a strong desire to serve their clients, so they continued to work for the agency in hopes that parity would eventually be achieved. After several years of lobbying and two directors later, a substantial increase in budget was received by the agency so that salaries could be increased. The director then had to decide how to award the increases. A scale was devised that gave the newest employees the greatest increases, and as time with the agency increased, a lesser percentage of a raise was awarded resulting in quite a large discrepancy between the new employees and those who had been with the agency several years. This perceived unfairness created low morale among those with seniority at the agency.

The reasoning that was given was that the agency wanted to attract and keep new employees rather than reward the employees who had been loyal for several years because they were already emotionally invested in the agency and had been accruing retirement benefits; therefore, they were highly unlikely to leave. This decision seemed to penalize the employees who had stuck it out for several years in hopes of eventually receiving fair compensation.

Based on the examples in this chapter, what political perspectives do you think were at play in this scenario? Do you agree with the director's decision? Why or why not?

Drawbacks to Lindblom's (incremental) branch model are that important details may be missed. Furthermore, there are no real comprehensive solutions, and it is a conservative decision-making process that doesn't lend itself to change except at margins. Lindblom and Matland (discussed previously in Chapter 6) both have distaste for the rational-comprehensive model and prefer to focus on the final product – a workable, albeit not perfect, solution.

Wildavsky[5] took Lindblom's incremental decision-making model and applied it to the budget process. As for why the incremental model seems to stand the test of time, Wildavsky credited conservatism and "bureaucratic inertia."[6] The popularity of the incremental approach resonates with our inability to plan too far in advance. Wildavsky noted, "[G]iven economic volatility and theoretical poverty, the ability to outguess the future is extremely limited."[7] Thus, budget managers lean toward the traditional, easier to control, incremental approach when proposing budgetary changes.

Determinism

Within the field of philosophy, determinism serves as the antithesis to free will. In other words, human behavior is subjected to external factors beyond our control. Events fall into place one after another according to fate, rather than individual choice. With regard to fiscal administration, interest groups exhibit overarching influence in the determinist perspective. Public budgeting comes to be less influenced by individual budget managers and is guided in large part by external forces.

In an article on technology and international development aid, Jan Cherlet[8] notes that public officials often use determinism to instigate and justify change in directions they see fit, with scant attention given to the social or cultural context of the recipient. The danger of a unidirectional approach is the tendency to lose sight of local context. In other words, while the idea of a knowledge economy might be largely accepted in the United States, initiating a technology transfer to a developing country must mesh with the system in place to receive the distribution. Good intentions can go awry if we lose sight of context.

Domestically, federal farming subsidies are examples of determinism at work. When farmers are incentivized financially to grow (or not grow, as the case may be) certain crops by the federal government, the choice of how to manage their fields becomes unduly influenced by interest groups rather than their own personal preference or needs.[9]

CASE IN POINT: YOU DECIDE

You are the executive director of a nonprofit, no-kill animal shelter. Your organization is largely volunteer-driven and relies heavily on in-kind donations of food, toys, and other supplies. The budget includes necessary personnel costs, supplies (such as food and medicine for the animals, cleaning materials, etc.), publicity/marketing, and ongoing maintenance expenses for your aging facility. The organization's five-year strategic plan includes building a new shelter, but the most immediate need is donations for supplies.

A long-time volunteer and donor approaches you about making a significant gift for the new shelter facility. Wow! This individual will donate half the cost of the capital project before the end of the current calendar year in return for having the building named after their family. Some members of your advisory board raise concerns about one donor potentially wielding undue influence over the organization. Do you accept the contribution, and if so, under what terms? How might this change in your strategic plan time frame affect operations for the current year?

Satisficing

The strictly rational model of policy decision-making necessitates that problems must be well defined with clear goals. In addition, every potential alternative must be identified and evaluated, including cost impact, before final approval may be given for the one ideal choice. Put another way by Ariely, "Standard economics assumes that we are rational – that we know all the pertinent information about our decisions, that we can calculate the value of the different options we face, and that we are cognitively unhindered in weighing the ramifications of each potential choice."[10]

CASE IN POINT: YOU DECIDE

Many of the decisions that public budget managers face are difficult, because you have to make them with limited information. For example, when a new product comes out that has claims to be better than what you were using before, do you use the new product that may last longer but is slightly more expensive, or do you keep using the product you know? Imagine that your agency has the opportunity to purchase a new software program that is designed to streamline human resources processes – from hiring to benefits and even payroll. The cost of the software needs to be considered in light of the training involved, personnel time required to implement the new system, and ongoing maintenance.

Sometimes, the long-term cost reductions and time savings outweigh the initial expense and trouble, making the change worthwhile. If you were the human resources director, what factors would you take into account when considering this software change for your organization?

Although the rational model was en vogue after World War II, Herbert Simon offered a new paradigm in which to consider the policy process.[11] Simon is credited with coining the phrase "bounded rationality," which acknowledged three reasons why decision-making in the policy process is not rational. First, the cognitive power of the human brain is limited and incapable of determining every possible alternative to a given problem. Second, there is no such thing as "perfect information," meaning that the outcome of each potential alternative cannot be predicted. Lastly, depending on how, where and when a policy is enacted, there may be different and unpredictable changes in cost. With regard to his first point, Simon asserted that the best policy makers can hope for is to find a satisfying alternative, not a maximizing one. This practice of satisficing seeks to establish guideline parameters, rather than the necessarily ideal option. Simon's bounded rationality model meshes well with what has become known as behavioral economics. As Camerer, Loewenstein and Rabin explain, behavioral economics addresses the psychological undercurrents of decision-making.[12] It entails the study of small tweaks in the decision-making process and is inherently irrational, compared to traditional economic theories.[13]

Simon's second point is more adequately addressed by Lindblom, who claimed that the policy process is comprised of a series of minor, incremental changes over time, rather than radical overhauls.[14] Lindblom's notion of bargaining and compromise during the decision-making process hearkens back to behavioral psychology (which is the foundation for behavioral economics) and is focused on finding politically viable alternatives, rather than the singular rational choice.[15] Although we may desire to know the future and be able to evaluate all possibilities during the decision-making process, it is simply an impossible, irrational feat.

CASE IN POINT: YOU DECIDE

At times, public sector purchases at the local level are made to satisfy needs and wants, but at a price that exceeds the goodwill generated toward the city council. Often, the initial cost of ownership is offset by external funds like grants, and constituents are convinced that a new service is a great deal for the community.

For example, let's say the Urban Mass Transportation Administration (UMTA) offers a grant to pay a large portion of the construction cost of an elevated rail system for a metropolitan city. The constituents are asked to approve 30-year bonds to pay the local share of the construction cost. The project receives broad support, until the system goes into operation and the constituents learn they are also responsible for all of the ongoing operating and maintenance costs of the system, and those costs are estimated to be more than two times the annual cost of the bond debt.

What appeared to be a great asset ended up becoming a burden that the city could not afford to own and operate. In retrospect, if you were serving on the transportation commission for the municipality, how would you advise decision-makers? Keep in mind that the metropolitan area desperately needs improved mobility, and the community is generally in favor of public transportation.

Punctuated Equilibrium

The aforementioned bounded rationality model is the foundation for punctuated equilibrium theory. The notion of punctuated equilibrium – a theory prevalent in the hard sciences and often associated with evolutionary research – entered the public policy arena with Baumgartner and Jones' influential book, *Agendas and Instability in American Politics*.[16] In a political science context, punctuated equilibrium denotes the periods of stability in a society, coupled with interspersed episodes of unanticipated change.

In contrast with the commonly upheld incrementalist mindset, punctuated equilibrium may explain more clearly why some public policies remain largely unchanged for long periods, then are adjusted in knee-jerk fashion in response to a political stimulus or perceived crisis or major events – for example, the way the 9/11 terrorist attacks prompted the swift creation of the Department of Homeland Security.

Unlike standard models of policy change based on cyclical election cycles and incremental adjustments over extended periods of time, Jones and Baumgartner went a step further and suggested that decision makers are limited by their own bounded rationality and subject to cognitive and emotional limits.[17] Punctuated equilibrium theory suggests that stability and disruptive forces battle for dominance, and human behavior – specifically, our emotional nature – holds the primary influence over our decisions.[18] Therefore, this human element leads to fits and starts in the policy decision making process.

If incrementalism is a gently sloping hill, then punctuated equilibrium is a staircase, illustrated by policy shifts as periods of stability are interspersed with episodes of swift change (see Figure 8.1). The Internal Revenue Service's (IRS) treatment of Bitcoin and related virtual currencies appears to match up with the notion of punctuated equilibrium. On March 25, 2014, the IRS issued a guidance statement in the form of a Frequently Asked Questions list to address transactions using virtual currency.[19] The notice was clearly geared toward Bitcoin and similar virtual currencies, in response to negative attention surrounding the Silk Road black market drug bust and other criminal cases involving virtual money. The emergence of virtual economies has opened the door to digital business models and even new forms of currency, and policymakers are scrambling to keep up with the changing times. Consequently,

Which line drawing best represents incrementalism? Punctuated equilibrium? What are some key differences between the two approaches?

FIGURE 8.1 Incrementalism vs. Punctuated Equilibrium

virtual currency is one example of a punch in the otherwise slow-to-change arena of tax policy.

An important step of the budget planning process, regardless of which of the approaches mentioned above are put into play, has to do with evaluating revenue. The next chapter will explore taxation, debt, and related revenue options as they pertain to public sector budgets.

Notes

1 Ruhil, A., Schneider, M., Teske, P., and Ji, B. M. (1999). Institutions and Reform: Reinventing Local Government. *Urban Affairs Review, 34*(3): 433–455, 433.
2 Ibid.
3 Lindblom, C. (1959). The Science of "Muddling Through." *Public Administration Review, 19*(2): 79–88.
4 Howlett, M. & Migone, A. 2011. Charles Lindblom is Alive and Well and Living in Punctuated Equilibrium Land. *Policy and Society, 30*(1): 53–62.
5 Wildavsky, A. (1978). A Budget for All Seasons? Why the Traditional Budget Lasts. *Public Administration Review, 38*(6): 501–509.
6 Ibid., 501.
7 Ibid., 504.
8 Cherlet, J. (2014). Epistemic and Technological Determinism in Development Aid. *Science, Technology, and Human Values, 39*(6): 773–794.
9 Fields, S. (2004). The Fat of the Land: Do Agricultural Subsidies Foster Poor Health? *Environmental Health Perspectives, 112*(14): A820–A823.
10 Ariely, D. (2009). *Predictably Irrational: The Hidden Forces That Shape Our Decisions*. New York: HarperCollins, 239.
11 Simon, H. A. (1955). A Behavioral Model of Rational Choice. *The Quarterly Journal of Economics, 69*(1): 99–118. doi: 10.2307/1884852.
12 Camerer, C., Loewenstein, G., & Rabin, M. (2004). *Advances in Behavioral Economics*. Princeton, NJ: Princeton University Press.
13 Ariely (2009).
14 Lindblom (1959).
15 Howlett, M. & Ramesh, M. (2009). *Studying Public Policy: Cycles and Policy Subsystems* (3rd ed.). Oxford University Press.
16 Baumgartner, F. R., & Jones, B. D. (2009). *Agendas and Instability in American Politics* (2nd ed.). Chicago: University of Chicago Press.
17 Jones, B. & Baumgartner, F. (2012). From There to Here: Punctuated Equilibrium to the General Punctuation Thesis to a Theory of Government Information Processing. *Policy Studies Journal, 40*(1): 1–19.
18 Ibid.
19 Aqui, K. A. (2014). New Guidance Clarifies Tax Treatment of Bitcoin and Other Virtual Currencies. Retrieved from: www.journalofaccountancy.com/News/20149850.htm.

9

EVALUATING REVENUE OPTIONS

Part of the rationale for establishing a new form of government among the new American colonies was their inability, under the Articles of Confederation, to collect taxes across the board. Individual states could collect taxes, but there was no central treasury to oversee or administer funds at the national level. In *Federalist* 35, Hamilton explained the need for the power of taxation:

> There is no part of the administration of government that requires extensive information and a thorough knowledge of the principles of political economy, so much as the business of taxation. The man who understands those principles best will be least likely to resort to oppressive expedients, or sacrifice any particular class of citizens to the procurement of revenue. It might be demonstrated that the most productive system of finance will always be the least burdensome. There can be no doubt that in order to a judicious exercise of the power of taxation, it is necessary that the person in whose hands it should be acquainted with the general genius, habits, and modes of thinking of the people at large, and with the resources of the country.

This chapter will introduce revenue options for public budgets, including taxation, intergovernmental relations (shared services, grant making, etc.), and debt administration. This section will also tackle concepts such as deficits and the debt ceiling.

Taxation

From vehicles to apparel to drive-through coffee drinks, most "tangible personal property and taxable services" in the United States are subject to Retail Sales Tax (RST).[1] While the rate varies from state to state and even within each state, the

United States remains the only member of the Organisation for Economic Co-operation and Development to prefer RST over an alternative consumption tax, the Value Added Tax (VAT). Unlike the point-of-sale nature of the RST, the VAT "… reflects a growing preference for broad based taxation of the full range of goods and services, as opposed to taxing specific goods."[2]

For both 2014 and 2015, the OECD average tax-to-GDP ratio exceeded 34 percent, and VAT revenues comprised the largest portion of consumption taxes, topping out at an average 20.1 percent of total tax revenue in 2014.[3] The VAT is a prerequisite for membership in the European Union, and at least 160 countries worldwide make use of this tax model.

Direct Versus Indirect Taxes

A direct tax, such as personal and corporate income tax, is based on the ability of the individual (or entity) to pay; in other words, a direct tax pertains to the contribution of the person/company to the economy. An employee works to earn a living, and a percentage of his or her income is taxable. Likewise, a corporation exists to make a profit, and a portion of that profit is also taxable. It is assumed (exemptions and deductions notwithstanding) that those who earn more will pay more, by virtue of their higher income. Such a structure is considered a pro-gressive tax, because those who make less are not burdened any more so than those who earn more. (Refer back to Chapter 2 for an introduction to taxes.)

Indirect taxes, by contrast, are based on usage of goods and services and are the same, regardless of the consumer's income. Consequently, indirect taxes are considered regressive in nature, because they penalize low-income consumers at a disproportional amount compared to wealthier ones. As O'Connell Xego and Govender noted, "… direct tax is a tax on income, profit and capital gains. VAT is an indirect tax that is levied on consumption, i.e. spending."[4]

Another term for indirect tax is consumption tax, and while the VAT is certainly not the only form of consumption tax (such as the aforementioned RST, as well as concepts like the flat tax, which applies an equal amount to all taxpayers, regardless of income level), it has quickly gained traction around the globe in recent decades. Even among VAT countries, however, there is no one system of implementation, "… given the large variance in factors such as the breadth of exemptions, multiple rates, tax base and general complexity of the model,"[5] as Hemels explained.

Value-Added Tax

Traditional sales tax is calculated and collected at the final point of sale in a retail transaction – for example, the purchase of a pair of jeans from a department store. The VAT imposes a consumption tax on every transaction – from wholesale to resale – in the production process of a good.[6] Returning to the example of the jeans, the VAT would be assessed on every step from the textile manufacturer to customer purchase, ostensibly including production of the denim fabric and stocking the product on the store shelves.

Among participating countries in the European Union (EU), efforts were made in the 1980s and '90s to harmonize VAT revenue and standardize rates between the member states. While some exceptions were granted for pre-existing policies, the EU has taken steps toward a more systematic implementation of VAT rates.

Proponents of a broad, flat-rate VAT claim that such a tax is neutral, because it should not alter relative prices. Opponents, on the other hand, assert that a VAT would drive up prices – and therefore, inflation – by taxing each phase of the manufacturing process. Like sales tax, a VAT generates revenue, which is another selling point in support for this method of taxation. However, states that already impose sales tax may have concerns about the VAT encroaching on their potential revenue through expanded sales tax rates.

While advocates attest that the VAT does not significantly alter consumer behavior, critics point out that the VAT is regressive because it does not take into account one's ability to pay. Other arguments in favor of the VAT include streamlining and stabilizing the tax code and thwarting tax evasion efforts.

An Unpopular Option for the United States

On paper, the VAT looks like a fair, neutral mode of taxation. It is collected incrementally, from primary producer to manufacturer to wholesaler to retailer. To recap, instead of charging a one-time sales tax at the time of purchase, the primary producer would have already paid a fraction of the tax rate when the material was sold to the manufacturer. Likewise, the manufacturer would pay a portion when selling to the wholesaler, and the wholesaler would follow suit when the retailer bought the finished product.

Like the RST, the end consumer still bears the brunt of the tax, but because the VAT is collected in stages along the production process, proponents attest that the VAT helps to close evasive corporate loopholes and retain more revenue for the government.[7] In 2015, the standard VAT rate hit 19.2 percent among OECD member countries.[8] The United States, by contrast, has no general sales tax at the national level; in fact, a handful of states do not levy sales tax at all. Because of this disparity, the VAT may be interpreted as promoting higher tax rates – a notion that is historically unpopular in the United States.[9] Still, sales and gross receipts comprise roughly a third of state tax revenue throughout the United States.[10]

Tax policy in the United States is more centralized and pluralist than comparison nations, and it is heavily influenced by interest groups, which falls under Adolino and Blake's "political school" theory.[11] However, no one theory of decision making covers any country entirely, just as seemingly disparate nations still may have similarities with each other. Adolino and Blake's "eclectic approach" emphasizes this point that national policy choices and the factors that play into individual policy development vary over time and by location.

U.S. Tax Policy

In contrast to highly regressive tax structures such as Sweden utilizes, the United States leans more toward redistributive taxes.[12] As aforementioned, the United States neither utilizes the VAT, nor do state and local sales taxes typically apply to groceries[13] – unlike Sweden and Japan, where consumption taxes are applicable to nearly everything except investments and exports.[14] Although a VAT has been proposed by Congressional representatives numerous times since the 1970s, both Democrat and Republican administrations have opted not to support it. Compared to other industrialized nations, sales taxes comprise less of total government receipts in the United States than those of other countries.[15] The United States depends more heavily on personal income taxes, with tax rates spanning 10 to 35 percent.[16]

Ironically, the United States charges nearly the same amount in corporate income taxes as Japan – well above the OECD average – yet, legal loopholes permit many United States corporations to escape paying the full amount (if any at all) of taxes owed. Such ambiguities become sources of contention with regard to maintaining domestic jobs in light of a global economy. Proponents of corporate loopholes argue that corporate income taxes are unacceptably high on the home front, then businesses may opt to relocate overseas where the tax climate is more amenable. Such moves potentially cost domestic jobs as well as potential corporate income tax revenue.

Taxation Challenges in the Digital Age

In traditional sales and purchases scenarios, the VAT is but one of several consumption-based taxes for decision makers to consider. However, in the globalized, digital society in which we live today, commerce looks more like bytes than it does baubles. Policy makers not only have to consider the mode of taxation for retail sales, but in this electronic age, they must also consider what constitutes a purchase, in the first place.

Technology has set a fast pace for local economies. American cities continue to evolve from industrial to hi-tech. Economic development at the local level became increasingly important as federal government disengagement of the 1980s meant that local governments had to be responsible for their own growth. Local economic development is undergirded by the city's tax base – largely through property tax and corporate incentives to boost commercial presence. Soft factors including workforce training, parks, and recreation also add to a community's appeal and drive economic development through tourism. Unlike previous generations whose economic well-being was calculated in terms of manufacturing and industrial products created and sold, the economy of the new millennium may be defined in general terms as not only the production and distribution of goods and services, but perhaps most notable of all, knowledge and information.[17]

Knowledge and information do not carry price tags like tangible products do; therefore, calculating the value of such abstract merchandise within the "knowledge economy" becomes a more complex endeavor than traditional sales and income tax models.[18] The process of assessing taxes on revenue from intangible goods becomes more complicated when the exchange of knowledge and information takes place across national borders.[19] The advent of virtual currencies used in game software and other synthetic environments confounds the issue even further.[20]

Technological advances in recent years have created not only a global economy, but also an entirely digital one. Synthetic environments – or virtual worlds – have grown so quickly that traditional tax policy structures are inadequate to address the emerging issues of these digital environments. In addition to the current discussion concerning fiscal policies, virtual worlds have repercussions in regulatory fields such as intellectual property, privacy, child safety, information security, and gaming guidelines.

For a more in-depth discussion of technology and innovation within the global economy, see Chapter 13. Next, we will switch gears from taxation to consider other ways of managing revenue, including debt administration.

Debt Administration

Susan Combs, former Texas Comptroller of Public Accounts, addressed a group of higher education leaders in 2011 to explain how the 12th largest economy in the world, the State of Texas, was striving to recover from the Great Recession.[21] Combs offered three options for balancing the state budget: cut spending, defer spending, and dip into the Rainy Day Fund – a reserve supply to address unexpected or emergency needs. The federal government does not have a Rainy Day Fund, so to speak. Its equivalent is the national debt – rather than dip into savings, the federal government borrows more money. The debt ceiling is the amount of money Congress permits the federal government to borrow. Month-to-month, the amount of money the government spends beyond what is budgeted is referred to as the federal deficit.

Recession Recovery and Deficit

As of spring 2017, new home sales were back to pre-recession figures of a decade ago, and the stock market had reached record highs.[22] Although the U.S. economy appears to be on the upswing, the country has continued on a spending spree that would have driven the typical family into bankruptcy by now. According to Fiscal Year 2015 tax returns filed with the IRS, the median U.S. adjusted gross income in 2014 was $38,171.[23] If the current average deficit-to-receipt ratio of the federal government were applied to this average individual, the person in the given example would be spending $10,596 more than they earned each year.[24] Put in other words, they would spend roughly 28 percent more than they made. With lines of credit piling up, such a blatant disregard for personal responsibility is unsustainable – it is a recipe for financial disaster. Bankruptcy is inevitable unless drastic lifestyle changes are made to curb spending, increase income, and eliminate debt.

Spending Cuts and Sequestration

Like the financially insecure individual in the above example, the federal government cannot continue to borrow its way to a balanced budget over the long term. The federal budget problems cannot be solved by imposing higher taxes alone, nor can spending be stripped to such bare minimums as to drive the country to a screeching halt. Solving the country's fiscal woes will require bipartisan compromise.

In order to reduce – and, ultimately, eliminate – the federal deficit, lawmakers must make a coordinated effort to reduce spending and build revenue. Budget cuts are often portrayed as a necessary evil, but if ongoing spending is not reined in, any proposed cuts will only suffice as a stop-gap measure.[25] On the flip side, increased taxation may not be the answer, either. Michael Mandelbaum, director of American foreign policy at the Johns Hopkins School of Advanced International Studies, put it frankly when he stated, "There aren't enough rich people to pay what we need."[26] With $192 billion outstanding in the monthly deficit,[27] increasing income will not solve the problem completely. Spending cuts must be implemented to constrain budgetary excesses and promote the country's long-term fiscal health.

Across-the-board cuts have been dubbed "the easy way out,"[28] but in an era of bi-partisan disagreements that threaten to shut down the government – such as the federal government faced in October 2013 – a proposal to reconcile the deficit with the most equitable impact possible is likely the only politically viable option. Automatic spending cuts, also known as sequestration, constitute a drastic but sometimes necessary interruption of out-of-control spending. Sequestration is not a new concept; in fact, the Gramm-Rudman-Hollings Deficit Reduction Act of 1985 garnered controversial attention back in its day for attempting to restrain deficit growth with the threat of sequestration if certain budget targets were not met.[29]

CASE IN POINT: YOU DECIDE

A regional hospital system recently cut back (and in some instances, completely eliminated) professional chaplain positions, with the rationale that local clergy could be recruited to come pray with patients from their respective faith groups at no cost. Critics of this decision attest that the hospital system failed to account for the things that professional chaplains are equipped to do, but which local clergy might not be able to offer. For instance, local clergy may not be trained to offer culturally responsive and interfaith care, crisis counseling, ethics consultation, or patient advocacy. Further, many patients and families have no religious affiliation, but still benefit from spiritual care by interfaith-trained chaplains, who come without a denominational or proselytizing agenda. Professional chaplains provide significant care to staff, often positively shaping employee satisfaction and retention.

Local clergy volunteers can meet some needs and reduce costs, but there may be other important functions that are either unaddressed or met inadequately. Bearing in mind the pros and cons of relying on volunteer clergy, how might the hospital system address its budgetary constraints while still serving the spiritual needs of its patients and families?

Intergovernmental Relations

Another term for collaboration between levels of government is intergovernmental relations; as such, it is an important offshoot of federalism. The "cultural school" of thought mentioned by Adolino and Blake[30] is particularly relevant when discussing collaborative efforts between government entities. Although all 50 states in the U.S. are accountable to the same federal government, they differ culturally – and, consequently, politically – in substantial ways.

CASE IN POINT: YOU DECIDE

Two rural communities recently decided to pool resources and share a fire department. In the short term, both municipalities have identified several benefits, in terms of community relations and cost savings, but they do not know what issues they may face down the road. What possible pros and cons can you envision with this partnership?

The case study above painted a picture of a nonprofit or public entity, such as a hospital, informally partnering with local community organizations (in this instance, local churches/clergy). While such efforts may help build public–private collaboration across sectors, entities within the public sphere also establish more formal partnerships.

Intergovernmental relations are evident at the local, state, and federal level, and although the ideal definition indicates a collaboration between government entities, intergovernmental relations are not always smooth and seamless. For example, counties may offset the cost of bus services on behalf of local school districts; in contrast, counties may pass down such costs as a burden for local municipalities and school districts to bear. On a larger scale, states may partner with (or disagree with, as the case may be) the federal government over border patrol services. The question of which entity would do a more effective job of protecting the border remains a contentious issue among southern states.

In the next section, we will turn our attention to the work of the nonprofit sector within the public sphere. As previously mentioned, nonprofit organizations run in many of the same circles as public agencies – and they often receive public funds in the way of grants. Yet, they are different enough to warrant special attention as a unique type of organizational structure.

Notes

1 Combs, S. (February 2009). Local Sales and Use Tax Bulletin. *Texas Comptroller of Public Accounts.*
2 OECD (2008). *Consumption Tax Trends 2008 VAT/GST and Excise Rates, Trends and Administration Issues: VAT/GST and Excise Rates, Trends and Administration Issues.* Paris: OECD Publishing. http://dx.doi.org/10.1787/ctt-2008-en.
3 OECD. Tax Revenues Reach New High. www.oecd.org/newsroom/tax-revenues-rea ch-new-high-as-the-tax-mix-shifts-further-towards-labour-and-consumption-taxes.htm.
4 O'Connell Xego, L. & Govender, R. (2009). VAT/GST and Direct Taxes: Different Purposes. In *Value Added Tax and Direct Taxation: Similarities and Differences*, Eds. Michael Lang and Peter Melz. Amsterdam, The Netherlands: IBFD, 103–124, 104.
5 Hemels, S. (2009). Influence of Different Purposes of Value Added Tax and Personal Income Tax on an Effective and Efficient Use of Tax Incentives: Taking Tax Incentives for the Arts and Culture as an Example. In *Value Added Tax and Direct Taxation: Similarities and Differences*, Eds. Michael Lang and Peter Melz. Amsterdam, The Netherlands: IBFD, 69.
6 Ibid.
7 Hemels (2009); Engel II, C. C. (2012). Revisiting the Value Added Tax: A Clear Solution to the Murky United States Corporate Tax Structure. *Indiana International & Comparative Law Review, 22*(2): 347–376.
8 OECD. Tax Revenues Reach New High. www.oecd.org/newsroom/tax-revenues-reach-new-high-as-the-tax-mix-shifts-further-towards-labour-and-consumption-taxes. htm.
9 Engel (2012).
10 U.S. Census Bureau. (March 21, 2016). *Quarterly Summary of State and Local Government Tax Revenue for 2016: Q4.* U.S. Department of Commerce.
11 Adolino, J. R. & Blake, C. H. (2011). *Comparing Public Policies: Issues and Choices in Industrialized Countries.* Washington, D.C.: CQ Press.
12 Steinmo, S. (July 1989). Political Institutions and Tax Policy in the United States, Sweden, and Britain. *World Politics, 41*(4): 500–535.
13 Exceptions include ten states, which charge full or reduced sales tax on groceries (as of the time of this writing). For details, see Figueroa, E. & Waxman, S. (March 1, 2017). Which States Tax the Sale of Food for Home Consumption in 2017? *Center on Budget and Policy Priorities.* www.cbpp.org/research/state-budget-and-tax/which-states-tax-the-sale-of-food-for-home-consumption-in-2017.
14 Ibid.
15 Adolino & Blake (2011).
16 Ibid.
17 Nordhaus, W. D. (January 2001). Productivity Growth and the New Economy. *National Bureau of Economic Research.* Working Paper 8096. Retrieved from: www.nber.

org/papers/w8096; Powell, W. W. and Snellman. K. (2004). The Knowledge Economy. *Annual Review of Sociology, 30*: 199–220. Retrieved from: www.jstor.org/stable/29737691.
18 Drucker, P. F. (1992). *The Age of Discontinuity: Guidelines to Our Changing Society* (8th ed.). New Brunswick: Transaction Publishers; Brinkley, I. (July 2006). *Defining the Knowledge Economy: Knowledge Economy Programme Report.* London: The Work Foundation.
19 Brady, D., Seeleib-Kaiser, M. & Beckfield, J. (December 2005). Economic Globalization and the Welfare State in Affluent Democracies, 1975–2001. *American Sociological Review, 70*(6): 921–948. Retrieved from: www.jstor.org/stable/4145400.
20 Castronova, E. (2006). A Cost-Benefit Analysis of Real-Money Trade in the Products of Synthetic Economies. *Info, 8*(6): 51–68. doi: 10.1108/14636690610707482; Chung, S. (2009). Real Taxation of Virtual Commerce. *Virginia Tax Review, 28*(3): 733–78; Beekman, N. A. (2010). Virtual Assets, Real Tax: The Capital Gains/Ordinary Income Distinction in Virtual Worlds. *The Columbia Science and Technology Law Review, 11* (August): 152.
21 Combs, S. (April 4, 2011). Speaking at Texas Women in Higher Education conference. Austin, Texas.
22 U.S. Census Bureau. New Residential Sales. Retrieved from: www.census.gov/construction/nrs/index.html.
23 IRS. Retrieved from www.irs.gov/uac/soi-tax-stats-tax-stats-at-a-glance.
24 Department of the Treasury. (2017). Monthly Treasury Statement of Receipts, Outlays, and Surplus/Deficit for Fiscal Year 2017 through February 2017. Financial Management Service. Ratio calculated based on cumulative receipts (billions) of $1,257 and deficit of $349.
25 Behn, R. D. (1985). Cutback Budgeting. *Journal of Policy Analysis and Management, 24* (2): 155–177; Naroff, J. & Scherer, R. (2014). *Big Picture Economics: How to Navigate the New Global Economy.* Hoboken, NJ: Wiley & Sons.
26 Mandelbaum, M. (March 31, 2001). Speaking at Laura Blanche Jackson Memorial Lecture. Baylor University, Waco, Texas.
27 Department of the Treasury, Financial Management Service. (2017). Monthly Treasury Statement of Receipts, Outlays, and Surplus/Deficit for Fiscal Year 2017 through February 2017.
28 Young, B. (April 4, 2011). Speaking at Texas Women in Higher Education Conference. Austin, Texas.
29 Stith, K. (1988). Rewriting the Fiscal Constitution: The Case of Gramm-Rudman-Hollings. *California Law Review, 76*: 593–670; Havens, H. S. (1986). Gramm-Rudman-Hollings: Origins and Implementation. *Public Budgeting & Finance, 6*: 4–24; Leloup, L. T., Graham, B. L. & Barwick, S. (1987). Deficit Politics and Constitutional Government: The Impact of Gramm-Rudman-Hollings. *Public Budgeting & Finance, 7*: 83–103.
30 Adolino & Blake (2011).

PART IV

The Third Sector

Nonprofit Organizations

10

THE ART AND SCIENCE OF NONPROFIT MANAGEMENT

The nonprofit realm is not immune to the theory and practice of public administration. This category includes a variety of charitable, educational, and advocacy organizations and although nonprofit organizations are not profit-seeking, they still manage human resources and often elaborate budgets. In fact, because nonprofit organizations are not taxable, they must rely on external funding through charitable contributions, in-kind donations of goods and volunteer hours, as well as grants in developing their budgets. Historically, nonprofit organizations have filled roles in the areas of professional standards, education and lobbying, industry standards, and accreditation. Fulfillment of these multiple roles of nonprofit advocacy boils down to one deliverable that cannot be overlooked: a clear and meaningful mission. An organization's message, particularly in dealing with legislative activity, must dovetail with the mission or vision of the group.

The Art and Science of Strategic Philanthropic Management in a Digital World

Nonprofit organizations (NPOs) are dependent on external funding sources to meet their budgetary needs. Regardless of whether such an organization represents an institution of higher education, social service provider, hospital or other nonprofit entity, the role of a fundraiser is similar to the position of a salesperson in the corporate world, except instead of selling products to customers, a fundraiser sells ideas to donors. A successful fundraiser seeks to align a donor's affinity, interests and capacity to the needs of the NPO.[1]

Advancements in technology allow nonprofit organizations to develop sophisticated data mining tools – often web-based – that permit fundraisers access to crucial information about the donors they intend to solicit. For example, property tax statements that indicate the value of homeowners' property are a matter of public record. By combining this information with other knowledge about the prospective donor, an organization can better determine the donor's capacity and inclination to make a major gift. Emerging technology is applicable not only to donor research, but such tools also open doors for nonprofit organizations to receive charitable contributions in a variety of electronic and alternative formats, including securities and virtual currency.[2] Understanding the creative and analytical ways (the *art* and *science*) of how nonprofit managers can harness technology for philanthropic purposes is the focus of this paper.

Perspectives on Management as Art and Science

Aesthetic Management (Art)

A manager who incorporates art, craft, and business as indistinguishable pursuits, rather than engaging in each task as purposely separate endeavors, might be called "Renaissance" or "Artisan."[3] One critical element of aesthetic management, explains author John Dobson, is decision-making on a holistic scale. Rather than considering economics and morality as two separate entities, for example, the aesthetic manager takes ethics into consideration alongside business. Dobson takes the discussion of business ethics a step further by referring to "value ethics" as being based on an individual manager's ability to discern and act ethically, rather than choosing between a preset understanding of ethical actions.[4]

The aesthetic manager aims for an Aristotelian form of well-rounded accomplishment complete with virtuous character in addition to ethical business practices. This type of management style is inherently artistic, rather than scientific, because it takes into consideration the individual manager's moral perspective and personal values. Furthermore, the aesthetic manager performs business functions without neglecting the art of his or her craft, and the same manager produces art while being mindful of the business aspects. Such a holistic view of one's tasks and decisions is a type of strategy that can be modeled from the boardroom to the battlefield.

The Art of War (Art)

While the concept of the Internet is still relatively new in the scope of world history, several timeless management principles can be applied herein. An ancient Chinese military strategist, Sun Tzu, expressed the need to focus one's resources and take initiative in order to overcome combatants' anticipated and unexpected maneuvers.[5] Sun Tzu's admonitions hold true in modern times because of the ever-evolving nature of technology.

Like Sun Tzu's warriors, a successful manager – whether in philanthropy or otherwise – must ascertain his or her team's strengths, focus on developing excellence and ride the wave of momentum toward higher and more challenging goals. Likewise, a manager must understand the weaknesses and strengths of his or her subordinates as well as peer organizations. Finally, a manager must take initiative to act in creative and innovative ways to position the organization in a superior position to its peers. This is especially true in the field of philanthropy, since multiple worthy organizations essentially compete against one another for a limited pool of funding resources.

Sun Tzu noted that "both advantage and danger are inherent in maneuvering for an advantageous position."[6] The mountaintop highs and valley lows of technological experiments are many, as any number of defunct companies that succumbed to the dot-com bust at the turn of the century can attest. However, a successful manager, especially in the fundraising arena, is not afraid to test the waters of technology to gain a lead for the organization while others are still wallowing in *we've-always-done-it-this-way* mode.[7]

The advantageous position for a nonprofit organization in a digital world is one that draws more traffic to websites, higher rates of online giving, and name and logo recognition. Positive, viral publicity through social network channels can gain attention for an organization that far surpasses what an organization could purchase commercially. When the target audience takes marketing into their own hands and shares positive news about an organization through social media, those constituents help to maneuver the organization into prominence.

As shown in Figure 10.1, below, online giving in recent years has thrived, despite the nationwide economic downturn in the late 2000s. The devastating earthquake in Haiti, to note one example, prompted a spike in nonprofit organizations receiving individual gifts of $1,000 or more online and set new records in philanthropic giving toward international affairs organizations – so much so that the 2011 figures were

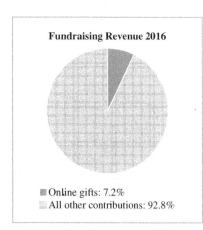

FIGURE 10.1 Online Giving Compared to eCommerce Sales in 2016
Source: MacLaughlin, S., Longfield, C., and O'Shaughnessy, J. 2017. *2016 Charitable Giving Report*, 5th Annual. Blackbaud Institute.

skewed when post-disaster giving leveled out.[8] MacLaughlin et al. also reported that tech-savvy organizations that were prepared to handle the influx of donors in the 72 hours immediately following the earthquake received the lion's share of contributions.[9] Social networks supplemented traditional media outlets to get the word out swiftly concerning the dire, immediate need in Haiti and greater Hispaniola.

In true Sun Tzu fashion, the most successful relief organizations were the ones whose strategy positioned them apart from the pack. A national philanthropic research firm even noted how the unprecedented outpouring of charitable support immediately following the 2010 earthquake demonstrated that "online giving is becoming the first-response method of choice for donors."[10] This statement has held true in the years following the Haiti earthquake, amid other natural disasters and emergencies.

Analytics and Performance Appraisals (Science)

With greater access to technology comes greater responsibility for accountability. Just as foundations and other nonprofit organizations must file annual Form 990 tax reports with the U.S. Internal Revenue Service, so too are pass-through funding sources like foundations and even private donors requiring more in-depth levels of fiscal and programmatic accounting by grant recipients.[11] In an uncertain economic climate, donors want to know that their expenditures are put to use in meaningful ways for the betterment of causes that they support. Excess funds are expected to be returned to the foundation for redistribution elsewhere, rather than used for extraneous purposes for the sake of using up the money before a deadline. Philanthropic managers must be fiscally wise and spend resources in ways that will garner the greatest impact for the program or cause, as well as stay in donors' good graces for the prospect of future gifts.

Meritocratic performance appraisal systems represent another scientific viewpoint of management. In a meritocracy, employees are hired on the basis of their abilities and evaluated according to objective performance measures, rather than more subjective traits such as personality and relational connections within the organization. Achieving a strictly objective performance review is easier said on paper than done the real world, however. After all, politics and other external factors influence and distort the system purposely or inadvertently.[12]

"Growing demands for planning and evaluation have placed a new emphasis on the need for sophisticated tools for applied research,"[13] noted Kozmetsky. Some external factors can be quantified, which opens the door for analytics as a management strategy. In nonprofit circles, in particular, data analysis plays an important role in evaluating fundraising goals and developing ongoing strategies. As Birkholz explained, "Analytics is a suite of metrical tools and techniques for understanding the past and projecting the future."[14] Donors' financial giving history lends itself naturally to quantitative analysis, but other influencing factors such as prospect affinity toward and participation in the organization, are more complex to quantify. Developing and using a metric system to analyze donor pools puts a scientific spin on strategic philanthropic management.

Competency Models (Art & Science)

If the purely objective practice of meritocracy were to add a subjective layer that considered the attitudes and habits of the human beings involved in various levels of the organization, the result would look like the competency models outlined by Lucia and Lepsinger.[15] Competency models take into consideration the behaviors of individuals in the context of the organizational culture, not simply their performance in quantifiable terms.

Certain management models, such as Mainero and Tromley's *Theory X* and *Theory Y*, attempt to structure organizations based on similar limited perspectives of human motivation.[16] *Theory X* represents the stereotypical micro-manager, one who grants no autonomy to subordinates and expects to have a hand in every function, not to mention every decision, of the organization. The *Theory Y* management style loosens the apron strings slightly, in that employees are expected to be somewhat self-directed, yet this model is still top-down in nature and heavily favors management over the ideas and input of subordinates. Performance reviews under these two management styles would center on how well an employee accomplished a set of objectives within certain parameters, rather than their value and contributions to the organization, as a whole.

The descriptions above are not intended to say that there is never a place for Theory X management. In the event of an emergency, for instance, encouraging autonomy and discretion among employees might not be the best approach. Rather, the agency needs swift, clear, and organized directions to ensure everyone's safety. Other highly structured entities, such as the military, function well under a Theory X style because of the strict chain of command inherent in the job description.

Competency models, likewise, represent a blend of scientific performance review with the art of the human element. In a management position, for example, Lucia and Lepsinger have identified more than a dozen core competencies that demonstrate proficiency for the position.[17] Such traits include the ability to delegate, mentor, solve problems, and engage in strategic planning. While these qualities are observable, they are still largely subjective and not easily quantified. Therein lies the art of management: to balance the human factor with measurable outcomes to create the ideal result.

Transformational Management (Art & Science)

At the root of management in any industry is the need to develop and properly utilize resources, human and otherwise. In his insightful 1985 text, George Kozmetsky advised future leaders to be mindful of the resources they are given.

"Tomorrow's managers of key institutions must understand that resources include science, technology, and information and that these are also assets for the solution of the nation's problems."[18] How fortuitous that more than three decades later, the same comments ring true.

Kozmetsky's remarks were geared toward the highly competitive supercomputer industry of the late 20th century, but his acumen is germane to emerging technology, generally speaking: "It is essential in improving our educational structure, fulfilling critical manpower requirements and enhancing our industrial creativity and innovation."[19] Even more so now, in this 21st century global economy, there is no room left in the corporate world – and certainly not the nonprofit sector – for stoic, old-school management styles devoid of technology.

If nothing else, the previous example of the 2010 earthquake in Haiti should serve as a wake-up call to nonprofit organizations: become tech-savvy or be left in the wake. The term *emerging technologies* implies that changes are in the works. Change can be frightening to an organization, but there cannot be growth without it. As Kozmetsky noted, "The management of change becomes the management of the creation and application of information technology that will enable individual institutions to achieve their goals."[20]

Technology demonstrably sparks an uptick in productivity across industries, and the nonprofit sector is no exception.[21] The key to harnessing this level of efficiency is understanding how – and being willing – to move from a traditional, paper-based, management style toward a far more encompassing transformational management model with technology at its core. As Kozmetsky explained, such a shift requires both creativity and innovation.

Creative and Innovative Management

Kozmetsky's groundbreaking work concerning transformational management has become more commonly known as Creative and Innovative Management (CIM). In his own words, Kozmetsky explained, "Creative and innovative management is concerned with understanding the state of the institution and that of society in order to improve each in terms of the general welfare."[22] Beyond traditional perspectives that may have been limited to the specific organization in question, CIM takes into consideration the use of technology and implications for society, at large.

> Technology is not simply an "engineering thing," a gadget or even a process. It is a national resource. Unlike natural and human resources, it is not consumed in the process of use. Rather, like a catalyst, it can be a stimulant; or it can be self-generating, as in fusion. The use of technology actually creates more technology.[23]

The traditional view of management, according to Kozmetsky, involves strategy, structure and the systems of the organization.[24] Strategy encompasses the future goals and direction of the corporation – or, in the case of the present discussion, nonprofit organization. Having a strategic plan to chart desired outcomes and next steps is important for a nonprofit organization, not only from an overall management perspective, but specifically for outlining fundraising priorities.

Likewise, the structure of an agency's organizational chart can either support or undermine the group's ability to fulfill its mission and goals. Without adequate personnel in place to carry out fundraising objectives, for example, other aspects of the strategic plan will falter due to lack of resources. Clear reporting lines help fundraisers understand to whom they are held accountable and support performance outcomes.

The third element of traditional management that Kozmetsky mentioned is the system, or functions, within an organization. For example, are fundraisers also expected to be event planners, or is another office responsible for such functions? Are academic deans expected to participate in fundraising endeavors, or is their function strictly scholarship and internal administration? Employees ought to understand their job descriptions clearly and how the functions they perform fit into the larger goals of the organization.

In addition to the standard elements of traditional management, Kozmetsky's transformational view adds the notions of style, staff and shared goals. To expand on the earlier topic of systems within an institution, it is also important to ascertain how the various functions fit into the organizational culture – or style – of the agency. Understanding the nuances and overlapping areas between job functions and the expectations of departments, at large, will aid an organization in developing an efficiently interconnected internal system, which builds camaraderie and encourages collaboration.

Kozmetsky also pointed out the importance of staff within an organization. Staff refers not only to the fulfillment of certain job descriptions by warm bodies, but truly to acknowledge the "people side" of an organization.[25] Placing a priority on staff entails making a vested interest in knowing who holds what role within the agency and being mindful of their potential and interests in moving up the ladder into more responsible positions over time. A manager who grasps this concept has employees who do not merely work in jobs; they build careers within the organization. In the fundraising world, such a distinction is critical, because longevity in a development position lends credence to the important art of relationship-building with current and future donors to the organization.

Another aspect of transformational management is the shared goals held by members of the organization at all levels. If first impressions are important to prospective students, potential donors and future clients, then the groundskeeper who maintains the front lawn of an institution's welcome center has as valuable a position as the President/CEO. Likewise, a maintenance worker who keeps the air conditioning system in optimal condition is as valuable as the department chair in the same building. When employees and managers across an organization aspire to the same goals, then everyone's role is not only important, but it also becomes interdependent on others to achieve the collective objectives.

Developing Human and Technological Potential

Like a strategic plan without the expectation of follow-through, administrators may spend months talking about being creative and innovative, but change comes with implementation. Kozmetsky identified two critical elements necessary to transform organizations. First, administrators must take advantage of the vast human potential in the midst of technological change; and secondly, organizations must cultivate CIM to meet the evolving needs and expectations of global society.[26]

Organizations that lack the infrastructure and manpower to implement comprehensive technology plans can still avail themselves of resources that will connect them with the digital world. For a nonprofit organization to succeed in developing the human potential that an institution needs to survive – and thrive – in this digital age, then administrators must recognize that technology should be a collaborative endeavor. Tapping into the human element is the *art* of management in a digital world, while the technology itself is the *science*.

CASE IN POINT: YOU DECIDE

Nonprofit organizations represent a private investment in the wellbeing of society. When philanthropic individuals and charitable organizations are actively engaged toward a common mission, unprecedented accomplishments can happen. At the same time, these organizations face greater competition for volunteer time and resources coupled with a heightened sense of accountability throughout the nonprofit sector.

There can be no doubt that technology is influencing not only the way we work and entertain ourselves, but also the way we manage. The overarching question is how to mesh the two: How do we, as budget managers in the public/nonprofit sector, navigate the digital world in which we live, while developing and maintaining a strong and capable workforce?

Adapt and Evolve Alongside Emerging Technologies

In recent decades, technology has supplemented, and even replaced, repetitive human tasks; today's global economy leans toward knowledge, rather than products.[27] A nonprofit organization must be about the business of sharing its mission and vision with the masses, and technology is the conduit to facilitate knowledge dissemination. The *art* and *science* cannot function in isolation from each other if an organization is to succeed.

"Economists have known for decades (and suspected for centuries) that such intangibles as ideas, knowledge, technology, scientific discoveries – call them whatever you want – drive the process of growth."[28] Although Romer's remark pertained to industry, such insight is valuable to the nonprofit sector, as well. Organizations that grasp technological platforms, such as the Network for Good's Social Giving modules, will be better suited not only to publicize their accomplishments but also to attract new donors via new avenues of giving and draw in such donors at higher dollar amounts, in the process.

Kozmetsky indicated that as organizations succeed in implementing the Creative and Innovative Management model, they will create value for their stakeholders. The personal goals of constituents will begin to mesh with the objectives of the organization, and ultimately, to the broader ideals of American society.

> Technology will have a definite impact on managerial decision-making processes. How much of an impact will depend on how well the linkages are structured among those who formulate the decision problems for solution, those who model the problems for specified telecommunication systems, those managers who make the decisions, and finally those who assess the accountability of the decisionmakers. These linkages were not required before, but their significance is essential now in order to adapt new concepts that technologies have made possible.[29]

The "linkages" to which Kozmetsky referred comprise the *art* and *science* of strategic philanthropic management. CIM offers a sound model for nonprofit organizations to emulate by capitalizing on the human resource potential within the organization as well as the ways in which technology can help the organization fulfill its mission.

Administrators of nonprofit organizations must realize that the science of technology tools and the art of human individuality need to work hand-in-hand to achieve overarching goals. Administrators in the nonprofit sector who are held accountable for their budgetary practices and performance outcomes by a board of directors and external stakeholders may be leery of jumping head-first into every latest and greatest technological gizmo to enter the market – and understandably so. However, the time for dabbling in technology has long since passed.[30]

A nonprofit organization that lacks the means to donate online via a clean and easily navigable website, is reluctant to engage in social media as additional means to interact with constituents, and/or considers technology a suffer-through task rather than a strategic management tool is failing to be responsive to donors and leaving money on the table.[31] In the next chapter, we will focus on endowed funds as a challenging but stable revenue stream for nonprofit organizations, particularly among institutions of higher education.

Notes

1 Birkholz, J. M. (2008). *Fundraising Analytics: Using Data to Guide Strategy*. Hoboken, NJ: John Wiley & Sons, Inc.
2 Murphy, M. K., Ed. (2000). *Corporate and Foundation Support: Strategies for Funding Education in the 21st Century*. New York: CASE Books.
3 Dobson, J. (1999). *The Art of Management and the Aesthetic Manager: The Coming Way of Business*. Westport, CT: Quorum Books, 125.
4 Ibid., 131.
5 Michaelson, G. A. & Michaelson, S. (2010). *Sun Tzu: The Art of War for Managers* (2nd ed.). Avon, MA: Adams Media.
6 Ibid., 69.
7 Birkholz (2008).
8 MacLaughlin, S., O'Shaughnessy, J., & Van Diest, A. (February 2012). *The 2011 Online Giving Report*. Charleston, SC: Blackbaud Institute.
9 Ibid.
10 Ibid., 6.
11 Birkholz (2008); Murphy (2000).
12 Smither, J. W., Ed. (1998). *Performance Appraisal: State of the Art in Practice*. San Francisco: Jossey-Bass.
13 Kozmetsky, G., Williams, F., & Williams, V. (2004). *New Wealth: Commercialization of Science and Technology for Business and Economic Development*. Westport, CT: Praeger Publishers, 6.
14 Birkholz (2008), 2.
15 Lucia, A. D. & Lepsinger, R. (1999). *The Art and Science of Competency Models*. San Francisco: Jossey-Bass.
16 Mainero, L. & Tromley, C. (1994). *Developing Managerial Skills in Organizational Behavior* (2nd ed.). Englewood Cliffs, NJ: Prentice Hall.
17 Lucia & Lepsinger (1999), 163.
18 Kozmetsky, G. (1985). *Transformational Management*. Cambridge, MA: Ballinger, 152.
19 Ibid., 131.
20 Ibid., 60.
21 Ibid., 5.
22 Ibid., 152.
23 Ibid., 143.
24 Ibid.
25 Ibid., 2.
26 Ibid., 5.
27 Romer, P. (2002). Foreword to *Patents, Citations & Innovations: A Window on the Knowledge Economy*, by Jaffe, A. B. & Trajtenberg, M. Cambridge, MA: MIT Press; Mokyr, J. 2002. *The Gifts of Athena: Historical Origins of the Knowledge Economy*. New Jersey: Princeton University Press.
28 Romer (2002), ix.
29 Kozmetsky (1985), 59.
30 Austin, J. E. & Wendroff, A. L. (March 8, 2001). The E-Philanthropy Revolution is Here to Stay. *Chronicle of Philanthropy, 13*(10): 72–74.
31 Burk, P. (2003). *Donor Centered Fundraising*. Chicago: Cygnus Applied Research; Warwick, M., T. Hart, and N. Allen, Eds. 2002. *Fundraising on the Internet: The ePhilanthropyFoundation.Org's Guide to Success Online*. San Francisco: Jossey-Bass.

11

ENDOWED FUNDS

Although the nonprofit realm is subject to similar accounting, reporting, and auditing practices as government agencies, these organizations have additional funding constraints based on their revenue sources. Nonprofit organizations receive charitable gifts in the form of one-time contributions, in-kind gifts such as goods and services, bequests and other planned gifts, and endowed gifts.

Endowment funds, especially in higher education, have been a point of contention with lawmakers over the past decade. Let's look at some of the concerns raised by legislators in light of the economic downturn of the late 2000s and how universities have responded to criticism about their endowments.

Unprecedented growth in university endowments in the mid-2000s prompted concerns about how well institutions are promoting access to higher education. Like all investment strategies, endowments are complex. Concerns about high tuition rates are not breaking news, but the issue escalated with the announcement in 2007 that American colleges and universities raised the most funds ever recorded to date ($29.8 billion). Private contributions to higher education had increased 6.3 percent, topping off the fourth straight year of growth. The top 20 universities raised a whopping quarter of total contributions.[1] The "haves" in the world of endowed funds were placed under a bright light of inspection to determine how diligently they were using the money with which they have been entrusted to serve students. *The Chronicle of Higher Education* pointed out, "As all that money has come in, some members of Congress have called for wealthy colleges and universities to distribute more of it to needy students."[2]

Endowment investment and spending strategies are the focus of much of the attention directed at wealthy institutions in recent years. The same investment scenario that indicates that the rich get richer because large pools of money earn exponentially better returns than small pockets of money also applies to college and university endowments. Institutions with substantial endowments have out-paced their less affluent peers hundreds of times over. Congress became involved in the rounds of inquiry beginning in September 2007, when the Senate Finance Committee called for a hearing about endowment growth. The hearing prompt-ed further scrutiny, and in January 2008, Senators Charles Grassley (R, Iowa) and Max Baucus (D, Montana) wrote a letter to 136 schools with endowments valued at more than $500 million asking about their endowment payouts and student aid practices.

"The Senate Finance Committee should have a complete picture before considering legislative changes," Grassley explained in an editorial column,

> That's why Chairman Baucus and I wrote to the colleges with the largest endowments to give them an opportunity to describe how they use their endowments and why, and how they distribute and publicize student aid. When we analyze the responses, we will proceed deliberately.[3]

Shortly thereafter, the House of Representatives passed the revised Higher Education Act in February 2008, which included verbiage about consistent spending increases for state universities. The House version of the Higher Education Act reauthorization also included a provision to increase reporting from institutions on tuition prices and data on endowment versus college costs.[4] Representative Paul Kujawski (D, Mass.) followed in Grassley's and Baucus' steps in May 2008 by sponsoring an amendment to the House budget, which, if passed, would have imposed an annual 2.5 percent tax on endowments over $1 billion. Grassley responded to Kujawski's recommendation by saying, "I don't want to tax colleges, but I do want to know more about how they are maximizing their tax-exempt status to fulfill their charitable mission of educating students."[5]

The most publicized piece of Grassley's idea was the proposed implementation of a minimum payout requirement. Private foundations are required by law to distribute five percent of their assets annually, and the suggestion posed by Grassley was comparable to the private foundation model. "Legislation to require the wealthiest institutions to have an annual 5-percent endowment payout remains a possibility, as does increased reporting about endowment performance and expenditures."[6]

Critics of the Grassley-Baucus plan questioned how higher education institutions and private foundations should be lumped together in the same payout model. Foundations are nonprofit organizations by design, and Grassley pointed to uni-versities' tax exempt status to explain the correlation. "Those tax exemptions involve a social compact: In exchange, colleges are obliged to carry out the charitable purpose of providing the best education to the most students at the lowest cost."[7] Foundations, on the other hand, are created for the sole purpose of funding charitable activities, and while they may incur administrative overhead expenses, their primary reason for existence is to give away money. Higher education institutions are based on a different model of revenue and expenditures. Certainly, colleges and universities have as their core mission educating students, but they also conduct research, job training, career development, community outreach programs, and a multitude of other functions in addition to teaching.

At their core, however, higher education institutions are still service organizations. Marion Fremont-Smith noted, "As a society, we have encouraged the creation and growth of nonprofit charitable organizations on the grounds that they provide unique benefits to the general public different in nature and purpose from those provided by government or the private sector."[8] Most colleges and universities are nonprofit organizations, but they are more akin to fee-for-service operations than philanthropic foundations. Higher education institutions range from community colleges to research incubators and include state-supported, private, and for-profit institutions. Comparing colleges and universities to private foundations makes little sense beyond the fact that most are nonprofit entities.

Chronology of Higher Education Policies

Harvard has been the beneficiary of generations of supporters since the original Harvard College was formed in the mid-1600s. As colleges both public and private proliferated throughout the United States, it became necessary to establish common guidelines by which they should handle gifts, investments and government relations. (See Table 11.1.)

In 1967, the Ford Foundation formed an Advisory Committee on Endowment, which was tasked with studying how universities managed their endowments. The foundation's ensuing report offered guidance for investment allocations with focus on maximum long-term total return.[9] The Ford Foundation study is of particular interest, since its recommendations laid the framework by which many colleges and universities organized their endowment investments, even to the present day. Unlike philanthropic foundations, which are mandated to spend at least five percent of their assets on an annual basis, colleges and universities that pattern their payout procedures on the Ford Foundation's model use a multi-year average, such as three years, rather than a more rigid annual formula. The multi-year method allows for greater flexibility to adapt to changes in the stock market and to project investment strategies over the long term. To better understand the policy changes suggested by members of Congress, it is important to begin with some basic principles of endowed funds.

About Endowments and How They Operate

Endowed funds seem complex, but at their core, such accounts exist to provide a permanent stream of revenue without draining the original value. Susan N. Gary explained, "Endowments are typically described as funds that maintain principle

TABLE 11.1 Benchmark Cases and Legislation on Higher Education Fiscal Policy

1830: Harvard College v. Armory – adoption of "Prudent Man Rule" over prescribed list of investments
1862: Morrill Act – land-grant colleges create compacts with state governments
1965: Higher Education Act – emphasis on educational resources and financial aid for students
1969: Ford Foundation Advisory Committee on Endowment – study offered guidance for investment allocations with focus on maximum long-term total return; the recommended three-year moving-average formula is still used by many colleges and universities today
1972: Uniform Management of Institutional Funds Act (UMIFA) – rules for handling endowed funds held by charitable institutions
1974: James Tobin (Nobel Prize in economics) made famous remarks about preserving endowments for generational equity
1983: Higher Education Price Index (HEPI) developed – inflation formula focused on colleges and universities
1994: Uniform Prudent Investor Act (UPIA) – governs investment conduct of trustees of private family trusts; first of three in a group of investment-related policies
1997: Uniform Management Public Employee Retirement Systems Act – governs investment conduct of trustees of public pension plans; second of three in a group of investment-related policies
2000 (amended in 2001 and 2003): Uniform Trust Code (UTC) – concerns enforcing terms of charitable gifts
2006: UMIFA becomes UPMIFA (Uniform Prudent Management of Institutional Funds Act) Texas HB 860 – more emphasis on investment management; third of three in a group of investment-related policies
2008: Higher Education Act reauthorization (February 7, 2008) HR 4137/S1642 – most recent update to Higher Education Act of 1965

and distribute income."[10] Understanding the concept of perpetuity and determining how much of an endowment's earnings should be spent are the crux of the endowment debate.

In this context, perpetuity means that an endowed fund should not ever run dry. It should be invested and spent in a manner that builds and reserves assets for countless years to come. Consider the case of Harvard University again. Harvard will celebrate its 400th anniversary in less than two decades. Its financial managers must not only consider the needs of currently enrolled students but also project the needs of those to follow decades from now, and try to do so in as evenhanded a manner as possible. Bajeux-Besnainou and Ogunc suggested, "The main objective of university endowments could be stated as providing adequate spending for current and future beneficiaries while not eroding the principal value of the endowment as they face an infinite time horizon."[11]

Just as student demographics, course offerings, and campus architecture contrast from school to school, the endowment levels at colleges and universities across the country vary dramatically. Sedlacek explained,

> The ongoing conundrum for institutional endowment managers and boards is deciding how much to distribute in any given period so that opportunities are protected for future students, and current students are not penalized – and to do this for the overall endowment and within individual endowment accounts.[12]

This statement raises the issue of what is commonly known as intergenerational equity, in other words, preserving the endowment at a level that means the same from one generation to the next.

Intergenerational Equity

Sedlacek explained that the term intergenerational equity gained footing in 1974, when

> ... Nobel prize-winning economist James Tobin made his famous assertion that "the trustees of endowed institutions are the guardians of the future against the claims of the present. It is their task to preserve equity among generations." This concept of intergenerational equity can be recast to say that future students should be given the same benefit of the endowment as current students.[13]

In essence, an endowment should have the same value in today's dollars as it did several years ago, and it ought to have greater value in the future to accommodate potential needs and adjust for inflation – otherwise known as real growth.

An endowed fund is not merely a savings account, however. It is designed to spin off earnings to support current needs. "[T]he goal is to maximize intergenerational equity. But providing a consistent stream of income to the operating budget and smoothing variations or fluctuations in finances also are important."[14] Concerns raised by members of Congress in the late 2000s assert that colleges and universities may be erring on the side of preserving their endowments at the detriment of current needs.

Because of its emphasis on guaranteeing future revenue, the notion of intergenerational equity "... implies very low tolerance for risk."[15] Colleges and universities are hesitant to spend too much of their endowment earnings in any given year for fear that the funds may not be available in the future. "Managers of endowment funds are particularly concerned about the downside risks of their investments because of their fiduciary responsibilities to balance today's spending and future growth of the portfolio."[16]

When a donor establishes an endowed fund at an institution, an expectation is understood that the monies will still be accessible years down the road. "By the principles of prudence and fairness, fiduciaries of endowment funds have the obligation not to discriminate between generations."[17]

Current gifts, as the name suggests, are exhausted immediately. For example, a donor may contribute $2,000 to a university for a current scholarship. The financial aid office at the institution will identify a qualified student, award the funds for the current academic year and deplete the account. In order for an endowed fund to contribute $2,000, on the other hand, the initial fund would need to be valued at approximately $30,000 to $50,000 – depending on the payout percentage of the university.

One of the frustrations expressed by members of Congress is that colleges and universities with strong endowments appear to spend too little of their endowment earnings.

> The trade-off between current spending and the growth of the endowment's corpus is a controversial issue as different approaches and dimensions might be brought to the analysis. The traditional view is that being impatient for the current spending might be detrimental to the chances of the future generations receiving the same "real" income.[18]

No two individual financial advisors implement exactly the same strategies for their customers. Likewise, higher education institutions often manage their funds with a team of investment personnel. Decisions on how to administer millions (or billions, as the case may be) of endowed dollars must take into account the volatility of the market and a sundry investment tools.

Tobin's principle of intergenerational equity "... is designed to permit a university to consume *recurrent* capital gains, but to avoid swings in income due to transient fluctuations in securities prices and changes in market discount rates,"[19] explained Woglom. This translates into a very complex balancing act that investment managers must play. The following section will review the blend of investment returns and fundraising that help to build a university's endowment.

Endowment Growth: Fundraising

As noted above, Harvard University, which has the largest total endowment of any higher education institution in the country, has borne the brunt of much negative press about endowment investment and spending over the past several years. An important point that is seldom recognized, however, is that roughly one-third of Harvard's operating budget actually stems from its endowment earnings. On the contrary, student-driven revenue and sponsored research support account for approximately 20 percent apiece. Considering that Harvard is a university known for its cutting-edge research, this finding is not insignificant.

A private university's spending comes from many sources, but, as a first approximation, the major sources of its funds that are spent educating and providing financial aid for undergraduate students are its undergraduate tuition revenues, its annual giving from alumni, other individuals, foundations and corporations that is available for current operations and its spending from its endowment.[20]

In Harvard's case, the latter category is of utmost importance. Figure 11.1 shows how Harvard's distribution of endowment earnings fares against other income streams to the university.

The funding categories listed above are several examples of what are called institutional funds. These accounts include not only philanthropic gifts but also tuition and other revenue-generating activities such as technology transfer and athletics. Institutional funds are monies held by an organization exclusively for fulfilling its charitable mission.[21]

Current gifts (expendable funds for immediate use) account for only about nine percent of Harvard University's operating budget. Yet, even these readily available funds are not necessarily undesignated. As Gary explained, "donor intent controls, so a charity must follow any specific donor directions for investment and management of assets."[22] Donors may specify particular uses for current gifts as well as endowed funds. To revisit an earlier example, a donor may contribute money for a current scholarship, to be awarded during the present academic year. Current funds might also be raised in support of a capital campaign or special event on campus. Just because the money is to be spent right away does not mean that the university has free rein to spend it as it pleases.

Merton addressed what he dubbed "…the interaction between spending and investment policies" in trying to explain how institutions operate fiscally.[23] "[A] standard approach to the management of endowment is to treat it as if it were the only asset of the university," Merton wrote. "Universities, as we all

Student tuition and fees (21%):
Sponsored research support (17%):
Endowment earnings (36%):
Current gifts (9%):
Other income (17%):

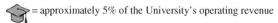

= approximately 5% of the University's operating revenue

FIGURE 11.1 Where Does the Money Go? A Snapshot of Harvard University's Endowment as a Percentage of its Operating Budget in 2016
Source: www.harvard.edu/about-harvard/harvard-glance/endowment

know, do have other assets, both tangible and intangible, many of which are important sources of cash flow. Examples of such sources are gifts, bequests, university business income, and public- and private-sector grants."[24]

The misunderstanding among critics of universities with large endowments is that such institutions are stockpiling funds that could be used for other purposes, such as tuition relief. While previous examples have shown that the role of an endowment is to grow the corpus of the account over time, the point cannot be overlooked that institutions are often restricted in their spending of donated funds. White puts the conundrum this way: "Still, at the end of the day, we must not forget that colleges and other charities are supplicants. Donors are the ones with the money, the leverage, and in many cases the vision."[25] Put simply, a university may have a list of priority fundraising needs, but if a donor finds an item further down the list more compelling than an item at the top of the list, then they may direct their giving accordingly.

An institution has the prerogative not to accept a gift that it finds unreasonable or contrary to its mission, but once a gift agreement is signed by both parties, changes can be very complicated and might even require authorization by the state attorney general. This type of legal intervention to change the scope of a gift is called cy pres. Fremont-Smith noted, "The origins of cy pres doctrine date back to the Middle Ages and Roman law as a means to permit charities to continue to make use of gifts, even if the original intent of the donor was unfeasible."[26]

CASE IN POINT: YOU DECIDE

Charitable contributions present a variety of opportunities for nonprofit organizations, including institutions of higher education, to consider their priorities in the short and long term. For instance, if a donor is interested in establishing an endowed fund, should we encourage them to set it up as undesignated? (Side note: this option is not typically preferred by donors.) Or, do we point them toward an endowed faculty position, which would help to offset our limited personnel resources? What about the need for steadily reliable research funding? An endowed research fund would ensure that important scientific inquiry could continue. All of the above represent credible needs of the university, but the priorities will vary by institution, and the choice is ultimately up to the donor.

Another example of determining needs in the short term versus long-range planning within higher education concerns the use of adjunct faculty. Appointing an adjunct faculty member typically costs less than paying a full-time faculty member an overload for teaching additional courses, and it is certainly cheaper than hiring a new faculty line. Think about the pros and cons of using adjuncts instead of full-time faculty. What could be some of the budgetary issues at play, as well as strategic planning priorities for the college or university?

To outsiders, it may appear that the university has its priorities off-kilter by erecting a memorial or planting new garden areas instead of putting funds aside for tuition relief, but the decisions are usually donor-driven. Institutions are bound by law to fulfill the intent of the donor, so if funds are designated for a specific purpose, the university cannot arbitrarily decide to pull those funds and use them for something else. Sedlacek pointed out, "A current misconception is that the size of an institution's total pool of endowment funds is the key determinant for achieving intergenerational equity and that therefore gifts to endowment can be treated in the same way as return on endowments. This is not true."[27] What a university can control are its undesignated accounts – funds that are not appropriated for a particular purpose. Undesignated, or general fund, accounts are the bottom line of the ongoing debate concerning endowment distributions. To better understand how endowed funds grow to the point of being able to dispense monies, the next section will focus on investment returns.

Endowment Growth: Investment Returns

Colleges and universities are high-profile entities within their respective communities, and with rising tuition costs at stage center, there is often confusion about how institutions manage their budgets. Lerner, Schoar, and Wang noted,

> Understanding the institutional qualities which allow some endowments to pursue unconventional investment strategies is particularly relevant because in a number of past episodes, schools pursued investment strategies that ultimately would have been successful, but were forced to abandon them when initial losses triggered media scrutiny and alumni complaints.[28]

Just as calls from Congress and education watchdogs have asserted that universities ought to be spending more of their endowment earnings, institutional investment professionals argue that mandating a minimum spending level could backfire and put the university in a risky situation during market downturns. Morrell explains the position of universities thus:

> Regardless of economic indicators, a general objective of investing is to attain returns consistent with risk tolerance – that is, the level of risk that an investor is willing to assume. An investor should never undertake more risk than is necessary to achieve desired returns nor try to attain returns that require more risk than necessary. The issue of risk is particularly critical for those of us who manage institutional investments. Unlike private investors, we must answer to a variety of stakeholders with differing goals and objectives from our funds. Each institution must establish an investment policy that fits its needs, but there are valuable strategies and principles that we share.[29]

Morrell raises an important point about investing institutional funds. A university may have, literally, thousands of individual endowed accounts for which it is responsible. The funds may range from a few thousand dollars to several million dollars apiece. As aforementioned, the accounts may also be designated for a particular purpose or available for general operating expenses.

Universities with substantial endowments have taken greater risk in recent years in their investment practices, such as foreign ventures and hedge funds.[30] Consequently, universities with larger endowments to begin with have, unsurprisingly, seen a more dramatic increase in their investment earnings. Lerner, Schoar, and Wang note that charitable gifts to endowment, returns on investment, and spending practices contribute to the changes in endowment size between institutions. Fundraising continues to be vitally important to the fiscal health of universities, but earnings from investments have played a significant role in the growth of many institutions' endowments.

Generally speaking, investing is a tricky business regardless of the amount of funds available. Prominent high-tech businesses have risen and fallen, seemingly overnight. The value of the dollar has decreased as developing countries around the world see glimpses of economic success. Morrell explained,

> The world of investing continues to be a challenge, especially with the global shift of economic power. While we have faced some of the elements of today's economic environment in the past, there is no roadmap for what's to come. Successful investors will be those who look ahead, incorporate tactical asset allocation approaches, and think globally.[31]

One of the ways in which universities compare endowment values to their peer institutions is not the overall dollar amount of the funds but the endowment per student. A public university system with tens of thousands of students should not be compared dollar-for-dollar with a small private college with only several hundred students. The amount of endowment per student may be a clearer indicator of a robust endowment than the overall total of the fund.[32] Although the concerns about mixing all endowed funds into supposedly unrestricted spending categories have already been addressed, the endowment per student calculation is worthwhile to obtain a more realistic understanding of the institution's endowment value than simply observing the total dollar amount.

The criticism of late centers on the extraordinary growth that institutions have realized with their endowed funds and spending practices that have not kept pace with earnings. In other words, "… endowment managers are giving more attention to portfolio management and growth of the endowment fund at the expense of spending rate policies."[33]

Because most institutions use the multi-year averaging rule that was discussed earlier, coupled with the basic premise that endowments are designed to grow over time to safeguard intergenerational equity, propositions that would require institutions to spend a set amount of their endowment earnings each year are more complicated than they appear. As a result of this averaging strategy and commitment to protect the real value of endowment funds, payout rates may seem low when compared to earnings.[34]

To further complicate matters, there is still the dilemma of institutions managing thousands of individual endowed funds. Gray described one approach to handling multiple endowed accounts:

> A charity holding more than one institutional fund may pool any or all of them for investment and management purposes. The pooled funds will be treated as one for purposes of applying the prudence and delegation rules, but they will continue to be considered individually for other purposes, including the rules governing spending endowments and modifying restrictions.[35]

For the sake of investment, as Gray noted, institutions may consider endowed funds as one large grouping, but the individual accounts must still abide by the donor intent. This brings up the important question of regulation.

Governing Policies

A consortium of state officials called the Uniform Law Commission meets regularly to devise accepted national standards for state laws. In 2006, the group approved revisions to existing institutional fund management policies at its National Conference of Commissioners on Uniform State Laws.[36] The new rule – dubbed UPMIFA for short – dictates how higher education institutions and other charitable organizations manage their investments. The Uniform Prudent Management of Institutional Funds Act (UPMIFA) is the new gold standard by which nonprofit organizations operate fiscally.

The former policy, UMIFA, had been in effect since 1972. Prior to then, the concepts of intergenerational equity and endowment growth were vague ideas to institutional fund investors. Before the approval of UMIFA, there was no consistent body of law to guide nonprofit decision-making concerning investment authority and the use of appreciation for endowed funds. Overly conservative and restrictive trust and investment laws in the various states caused institutional funds to be invested largely in low yielding bonds and fixed income instruments that delivered reasonably safe and dependable income but whose market value was constantly eroded by inflation.[37]

Only one word changed when UMIFA evolved into UPMIFA – the addition of the word "prudent." The implications of this single word are far-reaching, not the least of which is that UPMIFA allows greater flexibility than its predecessor. "UPMIFA updates the prudence standard that applies to the management and investment of charitable funds," explained Gary. "UPMIFA also modernizes the rules governing expenditures from endowment funds, both to provide better guidance on spending from endowment funds and to give institutions the ability to cope more easily with fluctuations in the value of the endowment."[38]

What this means to institutional investment professionals is that the pool of endowed accounts can be treated as one portfolio, so long as the purchasing power of the individual asset accounts is kept intact. It also means that investment personnel have greater leeway in their investment decisions (the "prudent" factor) and are not held to rigid guidelines such as the historic dollar value (HDV) benchmark.

Simply put, HDV refers to the face value of an endowed fund, including only dollars contributed initially and since the fund was established. HDV does not take into account inflation, investment earnings or losses or any other factors. "UPMIFA no longer uses the term 'historic dollar value' and no longer restricts spending to amounts above HDV … The intention of the change is not to permit unrestricted spending from an endowment fund."[39]

Finding the right balance is the key and the challenge to endowment investment. The changes put forth by UPMIFA are designed to help investors manage institutional funds with long-term vision. Agreeing where to draw the line between adequate spending for current needs and ensuring funds for the future has sparked passionate debate among higher education administrators and lawmakers. One university leader summarized the concern this way:

> Critics who attack how we manage our endowments – fueling calls for Congress to require a uniform minimum payout – have missed a key message: By not spending too much when the market is booming or too little when it is declining, colleges are better equipped to maintain our high-quality teaching and research missions over a long period of time. We are committed to spending our endowment income to ensure both quality and equity across generations.[40]

Regulations such as UPMIFA are crafted to help institutional fund managers avoid bad investment decisions and preserve intergenerational equity. The "what-if" factor sparks grave concerns among university administrators, as Sedlacek noted:

> When, as inevitably will happen, future market returns no longer are so favorable and inflation no longer so benign, an enforced 5 percent spending requirement will have the unforeseen result of forcing boards to spend imprudently large amounts from endowments that will then be weakened by poor investment results and eroded purchasing power.[41]

Then there is the question of how much college really costs. Massa confided, "For most colleges … the price we charge each student is less than our cost to educate that student."[42] In the midst of all the criticism concerning their endowment distributions, colleges and universities are waging an editorial column publicity campaign to tout their financial aid packages. Gutmann explained:

> Legislators and other critics who focus on the escalating cost of attending college should recognize that low- and middle-income students ... are not paying anything close to the sticker price – and that student aid at our colleges has often increased *faster* than our tuition.[43]

A study by Goldstein asked college and university presidents about change drivers in higher education. "Insufficient financial resources" topped the list at 60.5 percent. "The strongest response came in regard to the question of sufficiency of future resources. Respondents disagree strongly that institutions will have sufficient financial resources to meet future strategic objectives."[44] Managing an institutional budget is a delicate balancing act. As one university administrator noted: "Every dollar that we spend on aid from our operating budget is a dollar that we don't spend on something else."[45]

Much of the recent attention has focused on wealthy private universities. However, state institutions are not immune from scrutiny about their spending practices. Hyatt warned that:

> ... a growing number of public colleges and universities are evolving from primarily state-supported institutions to state-assisted or even state-related institutions. Amid the complexity of these scenarios, all these institutions can attest that developing alternative funding approaches raises critical questions that public colleges and universities must address.[46]

Ironically, some scholars have actually called for universities to withdraw less than the currently common spending rates, in the interest of ensuring intergenerational equity. Bajeaux-Besnainou and Ogunc cite research by Philip H. Dybvig from the 1990s wherein he advised institutions to shelter committed funds through lower performing yet more stable investment policy.[47]

Solutions/Compromises

Although the Grassley-Baucus plan and proposed Kujawski policy were not enacted in the mid-2000s, the endowment debate is far from over. All things considered, the most feasible solution could be considered a combination of limited government intervention and market-driven remedy. UPMIFA already requires documentation of prudent decision-making, but an additional step would be to enforce more stringent reporting obligations on higher education spending practices. Such transparency would, in turn, prompt stakeholders (students, education watchdogs, donors, etc.) to demand greater accountability from universities that are capable of allocating more funds for tuition relief.

An arbitrary tax on endowments such as the policy proffered by Rep. Kujawski fails to take into consideration the diverse structures of higher education institutions. For example, a tax on a moderate sized private university with an endowment of roughly $1 billion would be a different pill to swallow than the same tax rate on a large public university system with a multi-billion-dollar endowment.

Likewise, the policies proposed by Senators Grassley and Baucus were too stringent to be applied across the board. Gravelle found that higher investment returns on large endowments could permit those institutions to increase their payout rates without jeopardizing the total value of the endowment.[48] While Gravelle's observation is correct in one aspect – that unusually high investment gains could result in larger disbursements – it still neglects to address potential downturns in the market and the endowment per student ratio that is a more accurate representation of endowed fund value.

A more complicated solution might be to devise a formula to adjust endowment earnings against inflation. "Because higher education is a labor-intensive enterprise, educational input prices (as measured by the Higher Educational Price Index (HEPI)) typically rise more rapidly than overall prices (as measured by the consumer price index or CPI)."[49] The HEPI index might be a reasonable measuring rod; however, there are two key concerns.

First, HEPI is calculated annually, while most institutions still use a multi-year average to determine endowment distributions. Secondly, while HEPI has not decreased since it was first calculated in 1961, the most recent figures for the 2008 fiscal year show that HEPI did not keep pace with the Consumer Price Index (CPI).[50] This is an important finding, because as Blumenstyk notes, the CPI "is more heavily influenced by increases in costs for housing, transportation, and food,"[51] while HEPI takes a longer time to adjust to market changes. A formula that attempted to calculate HEPI alongside the CPI would invariably be faulty over time.

Colleges and universities already supply annual fiscal year data for various rankings and lists. Institutions also provide extensive data every 10 years for accreditation purposes. The report proposed here would span three to five years of data in the form of a survey report similar to the one requested by Sen. Grassley and Sen. Baucus, for example. An annual report would be unnecessary since most institutions use a multi-year average for their investments, not to mention the burden of compiling such data on a yearly basis.

This compromise would allow colleges and universities that are operating under prudent spending practices to educate pertinent parties on the good things they are doing and garner strong public support. On the contrary, should the reports identify institutions that are managing funds in what appears to be an unacceptable manner, these schools would find it necessary to validate their spending practices and justify imprudent fiscal policies.

Some colleges and universities already are taking voluntary steps in this direction. In the wake of Grassley-Baucus, institutions in Colorado, Virginia and California, for starters, agreed:

to negotiate a contract that specifies the performance goals the institution shall achieve during the period that it operates under the contract. Once again, financial aid and administrative flexibility is granted in exchange for increased accountability. This accountability is manifested not only through performance contracts, but also by monitoring tuition levels at public higher education institutions.[52]

Harvard, Stanford and other Ivy League universities also stepped up to the plate with drastic tuition cuts for qualified families, in the wake of criticism concerning their endowment management. Such action is proof positive that peer pressure and input from stakeholders can be a powerful motivator for voluntary change. Other universities may not be able to follow suit, but wealthy institutions that have unrestricted money available to use in such manner are now feeling greater pressure to apply those funds to expand access to higher education.

The solution proposed here strikes a balance between due diligence on the part of government regulations without mandating a one-size-fits-all policy that is bound to have more exceptions than perfect fits. Colleges and universities that uphold sound fiscal practices should not view this additional reporting obligation as threatening, because they have nothing to lose by publicizing what they are already doing well.

Notes

1 Wolverton, B. (February 29, 2008). Private Donations to Colleges Rise for 4th Consecutive Year. *The Chronicle of Higher Education*, A16.
2 Ibid.
3 Grassley, C. E. (May 30, 2008). Wealthy Colleges Must Make Themselves More Affordable. *The Chronicle of Higher Education*, A36.
4 *CQ Weekly Online*. (February 11, 2008). Comparing the House and Senate Education Bills. 394. Retrieved from: library.cqpress.com/cqweekly/document.php?id=week lyreport110-000002668484&type=hitlist&num=1.
5 Grassley (2008).
6 Ibid.
7 Ibid.
8 Fremont-Smith, M. R. (June 2007). Donors Rule. *Trusts & Estates, 146*(6): 10–15.
9 Advisory Committee on Endowment Management (1969). *Managing Educational Endowments: Report to the Ford Foundation.* New York: Ford Foundation.
10 Gary, S. N. (January/February 2007). UPMIFA – Coming Soon to a Legislature Near You. *Probate & Property, 21*(1): 32–35.
11 Bajeaux-Besnainou, I. & Ogunc, K. (2006). Spending Rules for Endowment Funds – A Dynamic Model with Subsistence Levels. *Review of Quantitative Finance and Accounting, 27*: 93–107, 93.
12 Sedlacek, V. O. (January/February 2008). The 5% Solution – Calls from Congress for a minimum 5 percent spending rate by college and university endowments ignore the core principle of intergenerational equity. *Trusteeship, 16*: 8–13.
13 Ibid., 8.

14 Ibid., 10.
15 Woglom, G. (2003). Endowment Spending Rates, Intergenerational Equity and the Sources of Capital Gains. *Economics of Education Review, 22*: 591–601, 591.
16 Bajeaux-Besnainou & Ogunc (2006), 93.
17 Ibid., 94.
18 Ibid., 104.
19 Woglom (2003), 591.
20 Ehrenberg, R. G. & Smith, C. L. (May 3, 2001). What a Difference a Decade Makes: Growing Wealth Inequality Among Ivy League Institutions. *Industrial and Labor Relations Working Papers.* Cornell University, 2.
21 Fremont-Smith (2007).
22 Gary (2007), 33.
23 Merton, R. C. (1993). Optimal Investment Strategies for University Endowment Funds. In *Studies of Supply and Demand in Higher Education.* Clotfelter, C. T. & Rothschild, M., Eds. Chicago: The University of Chicago Press, 211–242, 211.
24 Ibid., 213.
25 White, L. (February 22, 2008). More Money Doesn't Have to Mean More Problems. *The Chronicle of Higher Education, A29–A30, A30.*
26 Fremont-Smith (2007); Fisch, E. L. (Jan. 1953). The Cy Pres Doctrine and Changing Philosophies. *Michigan Law Review, 51*(3): 375–388.
27 Sedlacek (2008), 12.
28 Lerner, J., Schoar, A. & Wang, J. (2008). Secrets of the Academy: The Drivers of University Endowment Success. *MIT Sloan School of Management.* Working Paper, 1–27, 16.
29 Morrell, L. R. (December 2005). Investment To-Do's in Today's Environment. Retrieved from www.nacubo.org/x7391.xml.
30 Gravelle, J. G. (August 20, 2007). Tax Issues and University Endowments. *Congressional Research Service.*
31 Morrell (2005).
32 Gravelle (2007).
33 Bajeaux-Besnainou & Ogunc (2006), 104.
34 Gravelle (2007).
35 Gray, J. W. (2007). What's Different About *Prudent* Management of Institutional Funds? *2007 National Conference on Planned Giving.* Presentation given October 11, 2007 at the Gaylord Texan Resort, Grapevine, Texas.
36 Gary (2007).
37 Jarvis, W. (2015). Legislating the Normative Environment: Nonprofit Governance, Sarbanes-Oxley and UPMIFA. *Commonfund Institute.* 12 pp. Retrieved from: www.eric.ed.gov/contentdelivery/servlet/ERICServlet?accno=ED559280.
38 Gary (2007), 33.
39 Ibid., 34.
40 Gutmann, A. (May 23, 2008). Why Elite Colleges Have Sweetened Their Student-Aid Packages. *The Chronicle of Higher Education, 54*(37): A29–A30, A29.
41 Sedlacek (2008), 12.
42 Massa, R. J. (May 23, 2008). The New Student-Aid Landscape and College Admissions: a Report from the Trenches. *The Chronicle of Higher Education,* A30.
43 Gutmann (2008).
44 Goldstein, P. (2008). Looking at the Future of Higher Education. *NACUBO.* Retrieved from www.nacubo.org/x8417.xml.
45 Gutmann (2008), A29.
46 Hyatt, J. A. (November 2005). Redefining State Support. *NACUBO.* Retrieved from www.nacubo.org/x6979.xml.
47 Bajeaux-Besnainou & Ogunc (2006).

48 Gravelle (2007).
49 Woglom (2003), 595.
50 Blumenstyk (2008).
51 Ibid.
52 Hyatt (2005).

12

CHARITABLE GIFTS AND BEQUESTS

As Baby Boomers (defined here as those born between 1946 and 1964) are reaching retirement age and beginning to finalize their estate plans, recent changes in federal tax policy have come into the limelight over the past decade. The Pension Protection Act of 2006 and discussions at the federal level about repealing the estate tax, in particular, potentially affect giving practices of Baby Boomers. Using Anne M. Khademian's *Cultural Roots* model as a theoretical framework, this section first seeks to adapt the concept of family philanthropy to Khademian's model. Secondly, we will explore modern Planned Giving trends in light of evolving tax policy, with special emphasis on the Baby Boomer population.

Tax Incentives for Planned Gifts

On the heels of headline news concerning bankruptcies in the airline industry and the dearth in retirement benefit plans held by other U.S. corporations, the *Pension Protection Act of 2006* (P.L. 109–280) was set into motion by the 109th Congress.[1] Backlash by union advocates and media pressure propelled the matter into the spotlight. Economic explanations demonstrate why this issue rose in the priority list to become an agenda item – from devastating stock market conditions in recent years to long-term labor trends of older adults.

In addition to reforming the way companies manage pension programs, the 900-plus page *Pension Protection Act of 2006* also itemized restrictions concerning economic conundrums that have received far less attention from the press than retirement programs, yet the issues still pose hurdles for those affected – specifically, gifts routed through private foundations and donor-advised funds to charitable organizations.

Establishing a private foundation represents one of numerous financial planning options for wealthy individuals and families. Foundations come in various shapes and sizes, from relatively small assets held by a family-based board for highly restricted purposes to national organizations that support multi-million dollar efforts to alleviate societal ills on a global scale. Regardless of their size or individual mission, all private foundations are considered nonprofit, pass-through funding entities and are required to distribute a certain percentage of their assets annually. Although the Internal Revenue Service uses formulas to calculate the necessary distributable amount, a general rule of thumb to follow is five percent.[2]

Although different from private foundations, donor-advised funds function in a similar manner, in that they provide a means for individual donors to guide their philanthropic dollars to preferred charitable causes. Donor-advised funds may be managed by a private foundation or other institution, such as a bank trust. Once the money is deposited into the donor-advised fund, the donor receives a charitable contribution receipt. From that time onward, the funds are out of their control. Although they may offer recommendations as to where the funds should be spent, the repository of the donor-advised fund is not obligated to fulfill the donor's request.

Private foundations and donor-advised funds both can be useful conduits for facilitating charitable donations, yet there are a number of sticky issues about which fund managers, donors and recipient organizations need to be aware. Two of the concerns mentioned in the *Pension Protection Act of 2006* include:

- Self-dealing: The use of foundation assets toward any financial transaction between the foundation and a disqualified recipient.
- Excess benefit transaction: Any transaction in which a disqualified person receives an economic benefit, either directly or indirectly, from a public charity.
- Foundations must be mindful of prohibited activities that would be considered self-dealing or providing excess benefits to the organization or disqualified persons. A disqualified person is anyone who exercises influence over a public charity, which includes foundation board members and staff, donors, financial advisors and even families of the aforementioned.

Foundations can fall into the trap of self-dealing in several ways, including (but not limited to) selling or leasing property, extending credit, fulfilling personal pledges or providing goods or services. It would be inappropriate for a foundation to sell property to a board member, for example, or to extend credit to a staff member's child. It is also forbidden to pay a legally binding debt on behalf of a disqualified person. For instance, a foundation trustee who personally pledged to give to a local charity may not use a foundation grant to satisfy the pledge instead of his or her personal funds.

The last example – providing goods or services – presents a particularly challenging situation. Anytime goods or services are received in exchange for the price of a ticket (or other perks, such as seat options at an athletics event), then the foundation and its disqualified persons would be receiving a tangible, economic benefit by using the ticket, and such a transaction is not allowable. Even if a donor wanted to pay out-of-pocket for the value of the goods/services received and then have the foundation pay the charitable portion through his donor-advised fund or a private grant, it is still forbidden. This example would be considered bifurcating (cost-splitting) and is treated as self-dealing. Another example would be if a foundation trustee wanted to give the tickets (or other goods/services) away to a family member or friend. This use of foundation assets is considered to be for private benefit, not charitable.

Recently, both the Clinton Foundation and Trump Foundation have faced allegations of self-dealing. Foreign entities and prominent business owners have made sizeable contributions to the Clinton Foundation, which could give the appearance of meddling, particularly during Hillary Clinton's tenure as Secretary of State under the Obama administration.[3] As of this writing, however, the accusations toward the Clinton Foundation have not materialized, and the charity continues to receive 4-star and "A" ratings by watchdog groups.[4] By contrast, the Trump Foundation has taken heat on multiple occasions for using foundation funds to make contributions in order to ameliorate a personal or business conundrum, including satisfying legal settlements.[5] Some states do not even list the Trump Foundation on nonprofit organization registries because of the severity of its non-compliance issues.[6]

CASE IN POINT: YOU DECIDE

The compulsory nature of the *Pension Protection Act of 2006* is designed to impede people from making personal gain from so-called charitable contributions. In the examples provided above, the foundation, fund manager and other involved parties would be in violation of the *Pension Protection Act of 2006* and would be subject to punitive action. As the Executive Director of a nonprofit organization that benefits from bequests and other planned gifts, how would you rein in the potential for self-dealing within your organization?

Cultural Roots Model Adapted to Family Philanthropy

Khademian writes that the culture of a public program begins beneath the surface in an intricate root system of tasks, resources, and environment, and when those roots are nurtured with clear management focus, they will grow into the key commitments of the organization.[7] Next, we will consider how the same factors affect families as they consider immediate and future philanthropic plans.

Common understandings by working together create commitments – the context to interpret and approach work – and commitments manifest as culture.[8] Khademian states that in order to manage culture, one must learn to live and work within it. Organizations are built on hierarchy, and culture communicated clearly about how things are or ought to be done can guide work without tight central controls. The family culture is remarkably similar, given the natural hierarchy of generations and the principle of commitment required for a family unit to function cohesively.

Cultural Root – Task

The task(s) of a public program – what the organization does – is the first cultural root in Khademian's model. While families certainly have numerous tasks from raising children to managing finances, the primary concern of the present discussion is regarding philanthropic decision-making in families. As Jaffee notes, "A family gains structural capital by generating a formal family constitution that defines agreed-upon procedures that govern how family members participate in managing their wealth."[9]

Nearly one in five high net-worth households use a family foundation as a vehicle for charitable donations.[10] Oftentimes, the children or grandchildren of the foundation's creators will serve on the board of directors and help guide the grant-making process. Subsequent generations also raise and contribute funds to increase the corpus of the foundation.

> We are in the midst of an era in which the potential wealth available for philanthropy and social investment is staggering. Part of the work of family business advisors is to work with families as they make this transition and engage in giving away what they took so much care to acquire.[11]

Cultural Root – Resources

In Khademian's model, resources include the training and background of personnel – the human resources available to the organization. For the sake of our present discussion on philanthropy, resources pertain to a family's current wealth or income, estate plan, and counsel from legal and development professionals. A study of wealthy families indicates that a small number of American households provides the most resources to charity.

> High net-worth households, those with incomes of greater than $200,000 or assets in excess of $1,000,000, represent 3.1 percent of the total households in the United States. This very small number of households has an enormously disproportionate impact on charitable giving – they are responsible for approximately two-thirds of all household charity in this country.[12]

Not only do these wealthy families give away more money, but also more of the families give – 98.0 percent compared to 67.3 percent in the country at large. "To every type of organization, a higher proportion of high net-worth households made a donation than U.S. general population households."[13]

Average families direct most of their philanthropy to religious organizations, but wealthy families put their resources to somewhat broader purposes:

> For the general population, the majority of donations are directed towards religious organizations. However, most high net-worth household donations are given to organizations that serve a combination of purposes, such as the United Way, or to foundations, funds, or trusts. High net-worth households also give a disproportionately larger percentage of their donations to educational and arts and cultural organizations.[14]

The available data supports the assumption that wealthy individuals give more, but the heart of the matter is *why* people give. Among high net-worth households, "good business sense" ranked 11th as a motivation for charitable giving, with only 27 percent. The top three philanthropic incentives included meeting critical needs (86.3 percent), "giving back to society" (82.6 percent), and reciprocity (81.5 percent).[15] Consequently, the adage of *to whom much is given, much is required* seems to drive more wealthy individuals than business motives. Later in this section, we will examine specific tax benefits concerning charitable gifts.

Cultural Root – Environment

Environmental influences in an agency include public perceptions of the organization and its history. Continuing with our adaptation of Khademian's model to philanthropy, however, external factors such as investment climate, estate tax regulations, and income tax contribute to the charitable environment. Earlier studies have demonstrated that tax incentives do not typically determine whether or not someone will contribute, but they are a factor in the size of a donation, particularly with major gifts.[16] Paulette V. Maehara, former president and CEO of the Association of Fundraising Professionals explains this point:

> AFP has always suggested that donors to nonprofit organizations – whether charitable or political – are motivated primarily by reasons unrelated to personal tax benefits. Tax factors may help influence a donor's decision, but taxes aren't why individuals give. People give because they want to make the world a better place, not because they might get a tax benefit.[17]

Taxes also play a role in what is sometimes called *progressivity*, or advancing toward better conditions. *Boston College Law Review* hosted the State of Federal Income Taxation Symposium: Rates, Progressivity, and Budget Processes in

2004, where this topic was up for discussion: "Some of the symposium writing advocates for increased federal taxation on wealthy taxpayers without structural limitations beyond those that might be necessary to avoid unwanted effects that higher taxation might have on economic behavior."[18]

Although only a quarter of donors are motivated to "leave a legacy" in their giving, we cannot rule out the impact of taxation when considering the environmental factors of family philanthropy. "High net-worth households responded that their charitable giving would mostly stay the same if the estate tax were repealed and would stay the same or somewhat decrease if they received zero income tax deductions for their charitable contributions."[19]

Tasks, resources, and environment comprise the three intertwined roots in Khademian's Cultural Roots model for public organizations. We have used this foundation to demonstrate how family philanthropic decisions (tasks) are contingent upon available resources and changing tax and investment environment. Next, we will explore the management focus and program commitments portions of Khademian's model.

Management Focus

When Khademian refers to management focus, she discusses the inward, outward, and shared responsibilities within an organization:

> First, managers must focus inside the public program on the application of resources and personnel and the understanding of the public program task. Second, managers must engage with the outside environment, making changes or offering support as necessary. Third, managers must understand that the responsibility of managing the roots of culture and bringing about changes in the integration of program roots is one they share with a broad range of participants both inside and outside of the program.[20]

The management focus of family philanthropy boils down to life expectancy, since so much of charitable planning involves estate gifts, which must also consider heirs and other beneficiaries. Interestingly, two major surveys provide seemingly contradictory information regarding generational giving. An extensive study by Bank of America reported that giving levels in both high net-worth households and the general population tend to rise up to age 70, where they begin to taper off.

The report went on to state:

> Age is often a predictor of charitable giving in the general population; however, age does not seem to be a strong predictor of the philanthropy of high net-worth households. Average total, secular, and religious giving increases with age until age 70. After age 70, average and median giving levels decrease.[21]

Yet, another report by Craver, Mathews, Smith and Company and The Prime Group, *Navigating the Generational Divide in Fundraising and Advocacy*, publicizes that Baby Boomers, with a current age span of early 50s to early 70s, give the most to charity at approximately $1,361 annually. Pre-boomers (those born before World War II) give $1,138 annually, while younger generations give $791 per year.[22]

One explanation for the discrepancy between these two reports may be the interpretation of generation time lines. The commonly accepted date range for Baby Boomers is 1946–1964, yet some say that the Boomer era ended as early as 1961. Generation X is often defined as those born between 1963 and 1978, though the range could be as broad as 1961–1981. Millennials, or Generation Y, arguably began in 1982. The overlapping timelines of these three generations are illustrated in Figure 12.1.

Khademian asserts that program personnel must understand and be committed to how the work is done. New mandates and new managers can create a climate of uncertainty. Likewise, heads of households (family *managers*) must consider many factors when making responsible decisions regarding disposition of the family's wealth. Like the organizations mentioned in Khademian's model, families also have personality, and unifying culture enhances performance whether in public programs or in the home. Therefore, the top priority of a leader is to mold and maintain a unifying culture.

Program Commitments

The outcome of Khademian's *Cultural Roots* model is the grouping of program commitments that grow out of proper management focus on the tasks, resources, and environment surrounding the program. Depending on the organization, it may have a singular, or central, objective that it is designed to achieve, or it may have numerous goals to fulfill. The commitments of a family philanthropic plan are ultimately the beneficiaries of the family's wealth. We will round out our discussion of charitable tax implications with an overview of modern Planned Giving trends.

Not all gifts are deferred until death. Many donors give substantial gifts during their lifetimes. One charitable gift annuity booklet put it this way: "Indeed, with

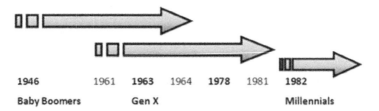

FIGURE 12.1 Overlapping Generations

some kinds of assets, the choice to make an outright charitable gift is the right one. There are, however, other ways to reach charitable goals and provide for personal financial considerations at the same time."[23]

Because 41.2 percent of high net-worth households have a provision in their wills for charity, it is important for nonprofit budget managers to understand some basics of estate planning.[24] An important term to understand regarding estate planning is *bequest*. "Bequests, which are simply gifts made through a will, have become an extremely popular method of providing long-term support for the charitable organizations that are so important in our lives."[25] Family philanthropy can be advantageous to both donor and beneficiary if planned for carefully:

> Charitable gifts and bequests are motivated primarily by the donor's desire to provide financial support for the charity. However, tax rewards can also be important. In certain cases, tax benefits can permit donors to give more to their charitable beneficiaries than they may have thought possible.
>
> Every dollar that is given to a qualified charitable organization through a bequest of other testamentary gift is fully deductible for federal estate tax purposes when certain legal requirements are met.[26]

Charitable remainder trusts and charitable gift annuities allow donors to give now, give later, and receive in the meantime, which allows the donor to realize tax savings immediately and in the future, when funds remaining after the donor's death become a charitable estate gift. Pentera, a planned giving marketing firm, describes the process to donors as follows:

> A charitable gift annuity is part charitable gift and part annuity. At the time you fund your gift annuity, we agree to pay you and/or another beneficiary a percentage of the gift amount over your designated beneficiary's lifetime(s). The payments are projected to last for the lifetime of the beneficiary(ies), with some of the funds left at the end for a gift to our institution.[27]

Another means of supporting charity through estate planning is the distribution of retirement benefits. More than 10 percent of high net-worth households have designated an IRA or retirement account for philanthropic purposes.[28] Because retirement benefits left to heirs are subject to both estate taxes and income taxes, estate planning with retirement funds is a rising trend.

> While your tax-deferred retirement-plan benefits are a great source of financial security during your lifetime, the downside is that the tax bill will hit in a big way if you leave retirement-plan benefits to your children, grandchildren, or other beneficiaries.[29]

Future Trends

Although discrepancy remains about which generation is truly the most philanthropic, there is no question that as the Baby Boomer population ages, more attention will be drawn to charitable gifts through estate planning. Be that as it may, Boomers are certainly not the only philanthropists. An encouraging finding in the research referenced in this chapter mentioned future trends for younger donors. As noted previously, young adults from Generations X and Y already contribute an average of $791 annually, and 56 percent plan to give more in the future.[30]

The roots of family philanthropy are planted deep, and as long as younger generations grow into the fruitful donors of their forefathers, then the culture of philanthropy will continue to thrive. As the next generation of donors matures, they are faced with a different economic environment than that of their parents – and vastly different from the world their grandparents grew up in. Today's global economy requires innovation and forward-thinking on the part of public administrators and nonprofit leaders. The next chapter will focus on agenda setting and innovation within this worldwide marketplace of ideas.

Notes

1 Davis, J. B. (2006). The Pension Plan Crisis: Municipalities and Private Companies Share Woes. *Compensation & Benefits Review, 38*: 52–56.
2 Internal Revenue Service. (2011). Taxes on Failure to Distribute Income – Private Foundations. Retrieved from: www.irs.gov/charities/foundations/article/0,,id= 137632,00.html.
3 Ashkenas, J. (Oct. 22, 2016). The Clinton and Trump Foundations are Vastly Different. Here's How. *The New York Times*. Retrieved from: www.nytimes.com/intera ctive/2016/10/22/us/elections/clinton-trump-foundation-comparison-criticism.html.
4 *Charity Watch*. Retrieved from: www.charitywatch.org/ratings-and-metrics/clinton-foundation/478; *Charity Navigator*. www.charitynavigator.org/index.cfm?bay=search. summary&orgid=16680.
5 NPR. Trump Foundation Admits to Violating Ban on Self-Dealing in Tax Filing. Recorded interview. Retrieved from: www.npr.org/2016/11/22/503052553/trump-foundation-admits-to-violating-ban-on-self-dealing-in-tax-filing.
6 Ashkenas (2016).
7 Khademian, A. M. (2002). *Working with Culture: The Way the Job Gets done in Public Programs*. Washington, D.C.: CQ Press.
8 Ibid., 43.
9 Jaffee, D. T. (April 2003). Six Dimensions of Wealth: Leaving the Fullest Value of Your Wealth to your Heirs. *Journal of Financial Planning*. 16(4): 80–87, 86.
10 Center on Philanthropy at Indiana University (2006). *Bank of America Study of High Net-Worth Philanthropy, Initial Report*. Indianapolis, Indiana: Center on Philanthropy at Indiana University, 57.
11 Jaffee (2002), 67.
12 Center on Philanthropy at Indiana University (2006), 3.
13 Ibid.
14 Ibid.
15 Ibid.

16 Assoc. of Fundraising Professionals. (November 13, 2006). Majority of Wealthy Unaffected by Tax Incentives, Not Interested in Leaving a Legacy. Retrieved from: www.afpnet.org/ka/ka-3.cfm?content_item_id=23844&folder_id=2345.

17 Ibid.

18 Kovach, R. J. (2006). Personal and Political Bias in the Debate over Federal Income Taxation Rates and Progressivity. *Akron Tax Journal, 21*(1): 1–32, 1.

19 Center on Philanthropy at Indiana University (2006), 57.

20 Khademian (2002), 65–66.

21 Center on Philanthropy at Indiana University (2006), 12.

22 Craver, Mathews, Smith & Company, and The Prime Group (2005). *Navigating the Generational Divide in Fundraising and Advocacy,* 58.

23 Pentera, Inc. (2005a). *The Charitable Gift Annuity: Guaranteed Payments for Life.* Pentera, Inc., 60.

24 Center on Philanthropy at Indiana University (2006), 57.

25 Ibid., 61.

26 Ibid.

27 Pentera, Inc. (2005b). *Charitable Remainder Trusts: Gift Plans of Choice.* Pentera, Inc., 63.

28 Center on Philanthropy at Indiana University (2006).

29 Pentera, Inc. (2005c). *Charitable Tax Planning with Retirement Funds.* Pentera, Inc., 69.

30 Craver, Mathews, Smith & Company (2005), 58.

PART V

Innovation and Globalization

13

AGENDA SETTING AND INNOVATION IN THE GLOBAL ECONOMY

When the economy is on the upswing, Americans tend to prefer small government and little interference; however, when the going gets tough, there is greater demand for government intervention in the economy. Local voters may contact their elected officials individually or en masse, and then the representatives in turn propose measures to support their voter base. Poor economic conditions spark discussions on agenda items related to the well-being of society, such as demands for more student aid support, increased funding for health and human services programs and tax incentives.

The entrepreneurial and individualistic spirit in the United States, for example, wields significant societal influence over the agenda setting process for legislation such as various iterations of the Farm Bill and tax breaks for the middle class. Lobbyists and political action groups specific to various causes and industries convey their constituents' expectations to decision makers.

Agenda Setting

In order for an issue to become part of the government's agenda, decision-makers need to be made aware of the problem, in the first place. Howlett, Ramesh and Perl define agenda setting in this type of problem-recognition context.[1] Adolino and Blake describe the hypothetical list of potential policy issues as a government's "systemic agenda," and the ones that warrant further attention become part of the "institutional agenda."[2] However, not all problems become action items, and the reasons why some issues make the agenda while others are set aside have to do with societal/cultural influences, economic conditions, political climate, and even the institutional structure of the government.

The political climate also plays an important role in setting the government's agenda. Political ideologies vary by party, and when one party has a majority say over another, such periods of time are referred to as political business cycles.[3] Like the corporate business cycle that rises and falls based on investment and spending practices, some political ideologies are pro-state while others are pro-market. Those who prefer market-based solutions tend to seek agenda items that take a hands-off approach to managing the government and let consumers guide the rudder. Pro-state advocates, on the other hand, will seek government-led solutions to apparent problems.

The institutional structure of a governing body influences its agenda setting practices, as well. In the United States, for example, it is highly possible – as witnessed in recent administrations – to have a President from one political party and a majority rule in Congress from an opposing party. Such divided viewpoints can create an impasse or stalemate, or it can prompt collaborative efforts and compromise.

Shared Governance

The professional practice model of shared governance has its roots in social contract theory discussed in Chapter 3. Under this model, professional practitioners join their administrative bodies in the decision-making processes of an organization. The American Association of University Professors (AAUP) adopted a statement in the mid-1960s concerning the importance of involving faculty in many aspects of university governance,[4] from personnel decisions to budget preparation and policy development. Shared governance has become widely appropriated within higher education and has diffused into other areas of the private and public sectors, such as the nursing field, where it gained traction in the late 1970s and '80s.[5]

Although the shared governance model is popular on paper, it can be controversial, in practice. In his book, *The Fall of the Faculty*, Benjamin Ginsberg raised concerns about administrators overreaching their authority under the guise of emergency management:

> Particularly aggressive administrators are prepared to confront and silence faculty resistance to their plans to establish new programs or reorganize old ones. One favorite administrative tactic is the claim that some fiscal or other emergency requires them to act with lightning speed – and without consulting the faculty – to save the university.[6]

The scenario mentioned above about power-hungry administrators could be avoided with an institutional commitment to shared governance and a firm understanding of the organization's mission. When problems become policy proposals which then evolve into political action, theorist John Kingdon likened

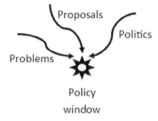

FIGURE 13.1 Kingdon's Policy Stream Convergence

the process to three streams converging into one brief "policy window" of opportune time.[7] In the illustration above, the perceived problem (an emergency) and politics (an administrator or group of administrators acting autonomously) took precedence over the proposal – in this case, involving other voices at the decision-making table. Kingdon's policy convergence streams are pictured in Figure 13.1.

On the contrary, when a hot-button issue (such as the aforementioned need for student aid support) also has the backing of parties involved, then two out of the three streams (problem and politics) are already in motion, making it more likely that the third stream (in this case, the creation of a policy proposal) will come to fruition. This path to agenda setting is known as inside initiation, because the visibility of the issue is already well known.[8] A similar tactic is outside initiation, which is designed to draw attention to a problem or spur debate about an issue.

To give another example of Kingdon's streams at work, a political actor may propose a policy based on his or her principled beliefs (which represents two of the requisite streams flowing), which then gives traction to an issue that was an unbeknownst problem previously (converging with the third stream). Such a problem-discovery method would fall under the mobilization model, because the political actor is the one bringing attention to the matter.[9]

CASE IN POINT: YOU DECIDE

In order for a funding need to rise higher in the priority list for an organization, the same three "streams" defined by Kingdon must converge. First, a problem (also known as the Statement of Need, in grantseeking circles) bubbles to the surface. Kingdon's streams can be illustrated by the following example. At my home institution, there is a need for an on-campus football stadium. The existing stadium is an older facility located across town, which is not only inconvenient for game goers, but it diminishes the campus spirit by separating game day festivities and discouraging alumni from visiting campus. Having a far-removed stadium is also a blight on recruiting efforts, when prospective student-athletes realize that they have to travel to and fro and do not have access to the same high-quality facilities that other peer universities offer.

To get the ball rolling, a proposal is brought to the attention of the administration – in this case, the pitch for a future stadium on the outskirts of campus, including cost and benefits analysis for both the university and surrounding community. A project of this scope will merge into Kingdon's "politics" stream more quickly when there are positive reinforcing scenarios, such as a winning season, high profile press coverage and/or a lead donor stepping up with a significant gift commitment.

Once a lead donor commits to the project, momentum builds and encourages other donors to get on board and support the endeavor. Unfortunately, this mode of fundraising can sometimes result in the decision making model knows as the Garbage Can Alternative. If an organization's priorities are guided by donor preferences more than by a cohesive strategic plan, then the Development team may flounder and not know the best project toward which to invest their time and energy. Because priorities can be swayed by lead support, the decision making shifts to participants (in this case, donors). Creating a donor-centered fundraising effort is important for a nonprofit organization to maintain good relationships with constituents, but we must also be mindful of mission creep and keep the organization on target to reach its institutional objectives.

As a member of the Development team, how would you communicate this prioritization strategy to concerned stakeholders who may have no interest whatsoever in a new football stadium and view the project as a misappropriated use of funds? On a related note, what is the university's ethical obligation to its donors who want to support certain pet projects over other priorities at the university?

Globalization and Economic Policy

In the mid-20th century, the convergence thesis popularized the notion that industrialized countries tend to develop similar public policies, yet this model of agenda setting has received criticism for focusing too squarely on budget expenditures as a measure of comparison.[10] The four widely accepted factors that propel would-be convergence include analogous domestic priorities and competition between peer countries, as well as influences of globalization such as legal issues and the melding of economies.

On a similar note, Knill identifies two broad categories to explain policy convergence, which overlap in some regard to the four-part description above. Quite simply, he states that the causes that prompted policy action and the related factors that impact policy efficacy are the overarching influencing factors of policy convergence.[11] Knill also recommends an even more thorough definition of policy convergence, to include distinctions between policy transfer – that is, knowledge and ideas that comprise the policy development process – and policy diffusion – the actual propagation of likeminded policies between political systems.[12]

The impact of globalization on domestic and international policy making cannot go unnoticed. In fact, transnational communication plays an important role as an external influence on the policy making process. Stone describes this dissemination of knowledge as flowing through global networks.[13] In addition to policy actors, the global economy of the new millennium also includes knowledge actors who provide expert opinions on policy matters of worldwide scope. These important players in the policy process serve as idea advocates and research critics; their networks reach within political parties and externally to international organizations. Knowledge actors are not limited to individuals; they can include professionally affiliated groups, non-governmental organizations and even transnational entities such as the World Bank.

The first two influential factors of international policy convergence – similar homeland issues and mimicry – play important roles in domestic and international policy development, as well. Kapstein describes one school of economic thought purporting that societies will strive to achieve their comparative advantage in the global economy.[14] Competition within the global sphere may compel countries to pursue policies that are similar in scope but tailored to their own assets. Kapstein's concept is called liberal internationalism, and it is inherently global as it seeks to bridge the gap between the *haves* and *have-nots* in the world economy.

For example, while communitarian-minded countries like the United States draw policy makers' attention to the need to keep domestic jobs, other countries like India have put the wheels into motion to be prepared to meet the demand for remote-capable jobs headquartered elsewhere. Technological adeptness and lower labor costs are two comparatively advantageous offerings that India puts on the global bargaining table. The policy environments both domestically and internationally play a role in how the respective countries manage the give-and-take of the global economy.

Globalization and Political Innovation

In order to keep up with the ever-evolving times, elected officials need to not only recognize the importance of, but also take stock of innovative ideas in the global economy. Bekkers, Edelenbos, and Steijn identify several ways in which innovations have permeated the public sector and the policy-making process,[15] but this section will focus primarily on the political and economic environment surrounding the election process and the growing use of social media as a strategic tool in elections and constituent engagement.

Election Climates

Elections are one of the key points of interaction between government and society.[16] In the weeks and months leading up to Election Day, incumbents and challengers highlight their platforms, make promises, present counterpoint arguments to the competition's claims and appeal to the public to cast votes in their favor. Elections are the primary means by which the public participates in the political system, and oftentimes, casting a ballot is one's only involvement in politics.

With the advent of radio, television and in recent decades, the Internet, elected officials are better poised than ever before in history to connect with their constituents en masse on a more personal level. Social media, in its varied digital forms, sets the stage for interpersonal communication between public officials and those they represent, and a myriad of real-time communication tools allow for a more intimate electoral process. The same phenomenon of competition that arises in the private sector is present in the election process, as well, and the public has come to expect both information and access to elected officials, and this demand creates the political environment for social media to reign.

Political Atmosphere

Bekkers, Edelenbos, and Steijn explain the premise for innovation in the political sphere:

> The need for public innovation can be defined as the search for new ideas and concepts, technologies, techniques and methods, forms, systems and procedures to create meaningful interactions between government and society in order to deal with a number of societal challenges.[17]

Social media overlaps each of the search terms mentioned above, because not only are numerous conceptual ideas prevalent in social media tools, but by its very nature, social media represents new technology and novel methods, procedures, etc. for disseminating information and facilitating communication between participants. In the election process, this two-way communication becomes all the more important as contenders seek ways to connect with and sway potential voters.

Choosing not to engage in social media is a high-stakes game, because rising expectations from constituents could lead to dire political ramifications.[18] An elected official who opts not to engage in social media is behind the times and liable to be perceived as unprogressive and antiquated. Indeed, as Bekkers, Edelenbos, and Steijn go on to say, "The ways in which governments are handling these problems not only affect their effectiveness but also influence the legitimacy of the governments themselves."[19] A technologically inept elected official is an ineffective representative of a tech-savvy public.

Innovations like social media not only help to lend credence to an election campaign, but such tools also help to build connections with the public. Within a representative democracy like the United States, scholars raise concerns of an "alleged crisis" in which constituents have lost a link between their mores and the individuals who have been elected to represent them.[20] In order for elected officials to overcome this perceived crisis, they must take initiative to reach out to the public on their level and in layman's terms.

Wellman et al. describe the importance of computer-mediated communication, such as social media, as an important complement to face-to-face interactions.[21] Because it would be impossible for elected officials to meet each and every one of their constituents personally and listen to their ideas and concerns, social media is a useful tool to glean the same feedback and offer information in a slightly removed, yet still relatively personal, way. This modified communication only works, however, if it is implemented as a conversational exchange and not just one-way.

Baxter and Marcella studied the use of social media during elections and found that during the 2010 UK General Election, candidates still used tools like Twitter and Facebook predominantly as information vessels, rather than harnessing their potential as interpersonal communication outlets.[22] This is an unfortunate over-sight of the vast potential of social media. By limiting outreach to one-way informational updates or news releases, candidates miss the opportunity to connect with constituents and potential new voters on a more personal, communicative level. A meta-analysis of the 2008 and 2012 election seasons by Shelley Boulianne suggested that although social media use in elections is generally perceived as positive, it has nominal influence on potential voters' participation.[23]

Such interpersonal applications of social media can potentially form a type of linkage between the elected and the represented. However, as Bekkers, Edelenbos, and Steijn noted, successfully building strong connections through open lines of communication poses a difficult task for the public sector: "One of the central challenges of public administration is to develop their own linking capabilities or to mobilize the collective capability of society and societal groups themselves."[24]

Governments tackle the challenges above by implementing the broad-sweeping goals of Information and Communication Technologies (ICTs), or e-government. The advent of ICTs meshes with the aforementioned notion of constructing linkages between elected officials and their diverse constituents. By transitioning government communication from the archaic, arduous, paper-pushing process of yesteryear into today's fast-paced, digital environment, governments employ new technologies to establish a system which is "... more open, more accessible, more responsive, more collaborative and more demand-oriented than government in the pre-Internet era."[25]

Collaboration begets unity, and unity helps to level the playing field within a democratic society. In a study of the democratizing nature of the Internet, Dylko et al. found that so-called "nonelites,"[26] or laypersons, exceeded their elite counterparts in the area of news distribution. While the elites dominated aspects such as news production, the study found that it was the everyday individuals who utilized their social media outlets to pass information swiftly and virally, from person to person and network to network. Within the climate of an election, the timely dissemination of information and opinion perspectives could be an influential factor in determining the outcome of a hotly contested race.

By using social media to share political news and opinions, the Dylko et al. study discovered that social media influence is not limited to the upper echelon; on the contrary, average persons had a notable impact in their ability to disseminate such information to a broader audience.[27] This round-trip pathway of the communication stream is especially pertinent to the present discussion regarding the use of social media in elections, because it spotlights the implications of such grassroots efforts on election outcomes.

Economic Atmosphere

Innovations like the use of social media in election races not only serve as politically valuable tools, but such progressive thinking also plays a role in economics and the way the public views spending in the public sector, particularly surrounding elections. Bekkers, Edelenbos, and Steijn noted that innovation "is a necessary condition for creating a competitive economy that will have a positive influence on environmental and social renewal."[28] The global economy is increasingly technological, and elected officials need to establish a digital presence, if they want to remain viable contenders as decision-makers in modern society.

Campaign spending is a hot-button issue right now, and for good reason. The cost to run a losing campaign at the state level can add up to tens of millions of dollars. At the national level, the figures are even more astounding. The Federal Election Commission reported contributions to Barack Obama's 2012 presidential campaign in excess of $722 million.[29] Comparatively, Mitt Romney raised more than $447 million. Fast-forward to 2016, when Hillary Clinton raised nearly $564 million and ultimately lost to Donald Trump, who garnered $333 million. Collectively, Democratic Party candidates collected almost $800 million, compared to their Republican Party counterparts with just over $639 million. By contrast, Libertarian Party frontrunner Gary Johnson raised $11.6 million, and Green Party candidate Jill Stein collected $9.5 million.[30]

Social media has been touted as a way to rein in campaign spending by shifting focus from expensive advertising outlets like television commercials back to old-fashioned word-of-mouth (or word-by-typing, as the case may be) advertisement. The advantage, of course, is that modern word-of-mouth communication through social media can spread exponentially in mere minutes, versus having a conversation one-on-one with another individual.

In addition to putting power in the hands of voters to disseminate information, social media also holds potential for incumbents and challengers to "... stay better connected to their voter base,"[31] as Qualman explains. When a voter "likes" a Facebook page or post, or when an individual "retweets" a remark on Twitter by an elected official, it allows the politician to better understand his or her supporters in the social media arena and can help them gauge which issues are of utmost importance to their voting constituents.

Amid current concerns about ethical campaigning and transparency concerning campaign contributions, the use of technology may provide benefits beyond simply connecting with constituents and potential voters. Bertot, Jaeger, and Grimes point out that ICTs serve as "… a cost-effective and convenient means to promote openness and transparency and to reduce corruption."[32] Transparency is no longer optional in the knowledge economy, when information is so readily available, and for an elected official to be openly (and willingly) transparent can only boost their reputation in a field that has so often been tainted by corruption.

Metaxas and Mustafaraj analyzed the use of social media in sample elections between 2010 and 2012 and noted:

> Even more than in previous elections, we should expect that all candidates and political parties will use social media sites to create enthusiasm in their troops, raise funds, and influence our perception of candidates (or our perception of their popularity).[33]

As the information age becomes more accessible at higher speeds than ever before through emerging technologies, social media will likely play an increasingly important role in future election races in the United States and across the globe, as incumbents and challengers seek to expand their voter bases and increase the impact of strategic advertising using stretched (and highly scrutinized) campaign dollars. Social media as an innovative tool helps to level the playing field among voters, increasing the spread of information across socio-economic lines and offering greater access to a broader span of voters. Just as transparency has come to be expected in modern-day election races, so too has social media become a key outlet for elected officials to share information and build their voter base – and their campaign coffers.

Notes

1   Howlett, M., Ramesh, M. & Perl, A. (2009). *Studying Public Policy: Cycles and Policy Subsystems.* (3rd ed.). Oxford University Press.
2   Adolino, J. R. & Blake, C. H. (2011). *Comparing Public Policies: Issues and Choices in Industrialized Countries.* Washington, D.C.: CQ Press, 11.
3   Howlett & Ramesh (2009).
4   AAUP. Shared Governance. Retrieved from: www.aaup.org/our-programs/shared-governance.
5   HCPRO. History and Development of Shared Governance. Retrieved from: www.hcpro.com/NRS-266847-975/From-the-staff-development-bookshelf-History-and-development-of-shared-governance.html.

6 Ginsberg, B. (2011). *The Fall of the Faculty*. New York: Oxford University Press, 9.

7 Kingdon, J. W. (1984). *Agendas, Alternatives and Public Policies*. Boston: Little, Brown.

8 Adolino & Blake (2011).

9 Ibid.

10 Ibid.

11 Knill, C. (October 2005). Introduction: Cross-national Policy Convergence: Concepts, Approaches and Explanatory Factors. *Journal of European Public Policy, 12*(5): 764–774.

12 Ibid.

13 Stone, D. (January 2002). Introduction: Global Knowledge and Advocacy Networks. *Global Networks, 2*(1): 1–11.

14 Kapstein, E. B. (2007). *Economic Justice in an Unfair World: Toward a Level Playing Field*. Princeton, NJ: Princeton University Press.

15 Bekkers, V., Edelenbos, J. & Steijn, B. Eds. (2011). *Innovation in the Public Sector: Linking Capacity and Leadership* [ebook version]. New York: Palgrave Macmillan.

16 Ibid.

17 Ibid. Chapter 1, Section *Lost Connections and Linking Capabilities*. Para. 1.

18 Ibid. Chapter 1, Section *The Innovation Challenge of the Public Sector*. Para. 4.

19 Ibid.

20 Ibid. Chapter 1, Section *The Alleged Crisis of Representative Democracy*. Para. 4.

21 Wellman, B., Salaff, J., Dimitrova, D., et al. (1996). Computer Networks as Social Networks: Collaborative Work, Telework, and Virtual Community. *Annual Review of Sociology. 22*: 213–238.

22 Baxter, G. & Marcella, R. (June 2012). Does Scotland "Like" This? Social Media Use by Political Parties and Candidates in Scotland during the 2010 UK General Election Campaign. *Libri, 62*: 109–124.

23 Boulianne, S. (2015). Social Media Use and Participation: A Meta-analysis of Current Research. *Information, Communication & Society, 18*: 524–538.

24 Ibid. Chapter 1, Section *Linking Capacity: Connecting "Government"*. Para. 1.

25 Ibid. Chapter 1, Section *E-government*. Para. 1.

26 Dylko, I. B., Beam, M. A., Landreville, K. D., & Geidner, N. (2012). Filtering 2008 US Presidential Election News on YouTube by Elites and Nonelites: An Examination of the Democratizing Potential of the Internet. *New Media Society, 14*: 832–849. doi: 10.1177/1461444811428899.

27 Ibid.

28 Bekkers, Edelenbos, & Steijn (2011). Chapter 1, Section *The Innovation Challenge of the Public Sector*. Para. 1.

29 Federal Election Commission. (2013). 2012 Presidential Campaign Finance. Retrieved from: www.fec.gov/disclosurep/pnational.do.

30 Federal Election Commission. (2016). 2016 Presidential Campaign Finance. Retrieved from: classic.fec.gov/disclosurep/pnational.do.

31 Qualman, E. (2012). *Socialnomics: How Social Media Transforms the Way We Live and Do Business*. Hoboken, NJ: John Wiley & Sons, 287.

32 Bertot, J. C., Jaeger, P. T. & Grimes, J. M. (July 2010). Using ICTs to Create a Culture of Transparency: E-government and Social Media as Openness and Anti-corruption Tools for Societies. *Government Information Quarterly, 27*(3): 264–271. doi: 10.1016/j.giq.2010.03.001.

33 Metaxas, P. T. & Mustafaraj, E. (October 2012). Social Media and the Elections. *Science and Society, 338*(6106): 472–473. doi: 10.1126/science.1230456.473.

14

INFORMATION MANAGEMENT, SECURITY, AND WHISTLEBLOWING

The impact of globalization is far-reaching, as technology synchronizes the world and melts away formerly insurmountable commercial and communication boundaries. As a historical example, the U.S. Census Bureau[1] reported in 1989 that only 15 percent of U.S. households owned a personal computer. In the late 1990s, the Census Bureau added households with internet access to its survey. By the turn of the century, more than half (51 percent) of U.S. households owned a computer, yet still less than half (41.5 percent) had internet access. By 2014, 78.9 percent of American households had at least one computer, and nearly three-fourths (74.8 percent) had home internet access.[2]

Technology is a tool, not a self-contained solution. Technology can help to drive advancements, but even the most innovative ideas would be listless without implementation. As technology advances across sectors, there is greater demand for interoperability between systems.[3] Put simply, interoperability is the sharing of digital information between people and organizations. As Landsbergen and Wolken describe, clustering information improves effectiveness, efficiency, and responsiveness.[4] Say, for example, that local law enforcement agencies notice an increase in arrests for a particular controlled substance among young adults. By coordinating efforts and sharing information with area school districts, authorities can improve outreach and educational programs to warn teenagers about specific types of drug abuse, as well as help to hone juvenile law enforcement efforts.

Unarguably, technology has aided the international flow of information and commerce in swift fashion, but information technology in the public sector involves so much more than paying a local water bill online, emailing your state representative, or submitting an electronic Social Security report. Government entities at the federal, state, and local level have an obligation not only to serve the public, but also to protect their digital identities and financial data. In many cases, that protection comes in the form of secure websites and databases to shield private information from nefarious hackers and other thieves who would seek to steal someone's identity in order to profit financially at their expense. In other situations, however, the entity from which the public seeks protection is the government, itself.

Privacy versus Public Safety

The Fourth Amendment of the U.S. Constitution protects individuals from arbitrary investigation or confiscation:

> The right of the people to be secure in their persons, houses, papers, and effects, against unreasonable searches and seizures, shall not be violated, and no Warrants shall issue, but upon probable cause, supported by Oath or affirmation, and particularly describing the place to be searched, and the persons or things to be seized.[5]

The terms *search* and *seizure* carried tangible connotations to early Americans, when a government official might, at will, barge in and ransack a home in order to commandeer property or rummage around for information. Worries have heightened since the country came under surprise attack on September 11, 2001, about the government's use of emerging technology to secretly investigate individuals in their homes, in public, and even digitally.

In the month following the 9/11 attacks, Congress passed the Uniting and Strengthening America by Providing Appropriate Tools Required to Intercept and Obstruct Terrorism Act of 2001 (abbreviated "USA PATRIOT ACT") to better enable the federal government to deal with terror suspects, including investigation, detention and deportation.[6] Unbeknownst to most congressional representatives, shortly thereafter, the President furtively approved efforts by the National Security Agency (NSA) to surreptitiously monitor telephone calls and e-mail correspondence between affiliates of al Qaeda and other terrorist groups overseas and persons stateside. Intelligence gathering is nothing new to the NSA, which was organized under President Truman's administration in 1952 and serves as the umbrella agency for 15 federal organizations in the intelligence community.

Bush's proposed surveillance program was authorized by Justice Department attorneys as being in full legal compliance and not requiring further endorsement by the Foreign Intelligence Surveillance Act (FISA), a 1978 law that delegated much authority to the Federal Bureau of Investigation (FBI) and the Central Intelligence Agency (CIA) regarding the domestic surveillance of foreign nationals.[7]

When a cover story ran in *The New York Times*[8] later that year exposing the secret surveillance program, the Bush administration stood by its authority to enact such a covert operation.

CASE IN POINT: YOU DECIDE

Cybercrime throughout the private and public sectors has been a problem for decades, and there seems to be no end in sight. The son of an NSA scientist once crashed thousands of computers on Bell Lab's network in 1988 with his "Internet worm."[9] Fast-forward to 2006, when an employee of the U.S. Department of Veterans Affairs took work home, and a laptop computer and external hard drive containing personal data on 26.5 million U.S. veterans was subsequently stolen from the staffer's residence.[10] More recently, the Internal Revenue Service was hacked in 2015 and again in 2016, exposing hundreds of thousands of tax payers' personal data.[11]

Part of the difficulty in dealing with cybercrime is the fluidity of the field. The Information Systems Security Association (ISSA) describes the difficulty of maintaining an adequate information security workforce: "Cybersecurity is a unique industry because it must identify and mitigate a variety of vulnerabilities in technologies that are constantly changing."[12]

As public administrators, we are caretakers of not only public resources, but also the public trust. What, then, should be our approach to combatting data breaches so we may ensure the security of our clients' and constituents' identities?

The 1967 *Berger v. New York* ruling overturned the longstanding 1928 *Olmstead* case, which had authorized domestic wiretapping by police. A key difference is that *Berger* categorized conversations as able to be seized. Justice Douglas likened the case to placing a police officer in every suspicious home, which he deemed a "bald invasion of privacy." Justice Black dissented, under the auspices that the Fourth Amendment applied not to searches of conversations but only to searches for and seizures of tangible things.[13]

Katz v. United States, a successor to the *Berger* case, is acclaimed with transferring the right of privacy from property to person and is frequently referenced as a champion case of the Fourth Amendment. In this case, an electronic listening and recording device was affixed to a phone booth used by Katz. Though there was no breach of his personal property, the ruling held that the eavesdropping was uncalled for. Stephen R. Viña wrote in the *Congressional Research Service* journal, "Not until the landmark decision of *Katz v. United States* in 1967 did the Supreme Court abandon its structural 'property' approach for a fluid constitutional framework that was to 'protect people, not places'."[14]

Viña noted in reference to the 1967 *Camara v. Municipal Court* decision, "In instances where the interests of the public outweigh those of private individuals … the Court has recognized 'specifically established exceptions' to the warrant and probable cause requirements of the Fourth Amendment."[15] Another example of the Supreme Court finding cause to lift warrant restrictions can be found in Justice Sandra Day O'Connor's dissenting opinion in *Vernonia School District v. Acton*. She commented that both the warrant and probable cause mandates can be lifted when "even one undetected instance of wrongdoing could have injurious consequences for a great number of people."[16]

The Bush administration received severe criticism for its surveillance program, but these issues are not limited to the 43rd President. In more recent days, federal agencies have attempted to forcibly compel private companies to release information on customers. The FBI-Apple encryption dispute,[17] for example, pitted Apple Inc. against the Federal Bureau of Investigation in a digital standoff concerning Apple's refusal to provide the FBI with software to unlock an encrypted iPhone. The case was unceremoniously dropped a day prior to the hearing because the FBI found a third party to hack the phone in question. The definitions of property, person, and place have evolved to include digital presence and cloud storage.

In another example of digital inquiry – this time with a warrant, but critics assert that the request is "unconstitutionally broad"[18] – the Justice Department demanded an internet hosting company disclose information about visitors to a website that protesters used during the inauguration activities of President Trump. However, instead of providing information on specific suspects, the data dump would expose more than 1.3 million web hits over the course of six days. Needless to say, the fight over privacy and surveillance is far from finished.

Whistleblowing

While the Whistleblower Protection Act of 1989 is geared toward identifying government misconduct, in a general sense, public budget administrators would be remiss to ignore the dangers of fraud or turn a blind eye to waste and other fiscal abuses within their organizations. The Occupational Safety and Health Administration (OSHA), to offer one example, provides an online portal[19] for employees to report a variety of workplace violations, including financial transgressions, and whistleblowers have broad employment protections if and when they report a concern.

A framework is not intended to be an end, in and of itself. Rather, it is the scaffolding upon which to build. Cybercrimes will continue to evolve, and nefarious individuals will continue to seek ways to infiltrate and sabotage our systems. Our role, as public administrators, is to establish ethical parameters for decision-making within our organizations and do everything within our power to maintain and ensure the public trust.

CASE IN POINT: YOU DECIDE

Robert MacLean was a federal air marshal who blew the whistle on the Transportation Security Administration (TSA) in 2003 after they issued a cost-saving measure to reduce the number of air marshals on long-distance flights, just days after notifying air marshals of intelligence suggesting that terrorist group al-Qaeda was planning additional hijacking attacks. The agency charged MacLean with disclosure of confidential safety policies, and he countered by pointing out that the TSA sent orders to air marshals using text messaging to unsecured phones. His case languished until the Supreme Court ruled 7–2 in MacLean's favor in 2015. Although ultimately reinstated to the TSA, MacLean lost years of seniority and was treated as a rookie employee.

MacLean's case highlights a number of ethical concerns, not the least of which is the TSA's use of unsecured modes of communication to pass along updates regarding national security. For our purposes in addressing ethical fiscal administration, however, let us consider the financial decision to cut back on the number of air marshals assigned to long-distance flights, on the heels of heightened security concerns. Given that hindsight is 20/20, if you worked on the budget team with the TSA, how might you have handled this situation differently?

In the following chapter, we will construct an ethical framework to assist public administrators in creating the kind of integrity-infused workplace environments where whistleblowing becomes unnecessary.

Notes

1 United States Census Bureau. (2001). www.census.gov/prod/2001pubs/p23-207.pdf.
2 United States Census Bureau. (2012). Computer and Internet Access in the United States: 2012. Retrieved from: www.census.gov/data/tables/2012/demo/computer-internet/computer-use-2012.html.
3 Landsbergen Jr., D. & Wolken Jr., G. (2001). Realizing the Promise: Government Information Systems and the Fourth Generation of Information Technology. *Public Administration Review, 61*(2): 206–220.
4 Ibid.
5 *U.S. Constitution,* Amendment IV.
6 Cusick, K. R. (2003). Thwarting Ideological Terrorism: Are we Brave Enough to Maintain Civil Liberties in the Face of Terrorist Induced Trauma? *Case Western Reserve Journal of International Law, 35*(1): 55–88.
7 Ibid.
8 Risen, J. & Lichtblau, E. (December 16, 2005). Bush Lets U.S. Spy on Callers Without Courts. *New York Times.*
9 Schell, B. H. & Martin, C. (2004). *Cybercrime: A Reference Handbook.* Santa Barbara, CA: ABC-CLIO, 3.
10 Vijayan, J. (June 1, 2007). One Year Later: Five Lessons Learned from the VA Data Breach. *Computer World.* Retrieved from: www.computerworld.com/article/2541516/security0/one-year-later–five-lessons-learned-from-the-va-data-breach.html.

11 Chew, J. (Feb. 10, 2016). The IRS Says Identity Thieves Hacked its Systems Again. *Fortune*. Retrieved from: fortune.com/2016/02/10/irs-hack-refunds.

12 Barrett, R. (June 18, 2017). Digital Organizations Face a Huge Cybersecurity Skills Gap. *Venture Beat*. Retrieved from: venturebeat.com/2017/06/18/digital-organizations-face-a-huge-cybersecurity-skills-gap.

13 *Berger v. New York*. 1967. 388 U.S. 41.

14 Viña, S. R. (May 17, 2005). Protecting Our Perimeter: 'Border Searches' under the Fourth Amendment. *CRS Report for Congress*. Washington, DC: The Library of Congress, 4.

15 Ibid., 3.

16 Blitz, M. J. (2004). Video Surveillance and the Constitution of Public Space: Fitting the Fourth Amendment to a World that Tracks Image and Identity. *Texas Law Review*, *82*(6): 1349–1481, 1360.

17 House of Representatives Judiciary Committee Hearing. The Encryption Tightrope: Balancing Americans' Security and Privacy. judiciary.house.gov/hearing/the-encryption-tightrope-balancing-americans-security-and-privacy.

18 Savage, C. (August 15, 2017). Justice Dept. Demands Data on Visitors to Anti-Trump Website, Sparking Fight. *The New York Times*. Retrieved from: www.nytimes.com/2017/08/15/us/politics/justice-department-trump-dreamhost-protests.html.

19 OSHA Whistleblower Protection Programs. Retrieved from: www.whistleblowers.gov.

PART VI

Application and Conclusion

15

DEVELOPING AN ETHICAL FRAMEWORK

As mentioned in reference to Svara's ethical triangle in Chapter 4, the decision making conundrum for ethical fiscal administrators hinges on the balance between principles, consequences, and virtue (or intuition). In this chapter, we will take the discussion a step further and consider the context for our own ethical framework. Using the Network of Schools of Public Policy, Affairs, and Administration (NASPAA) and the American Society for Public Administration (ASPA) as two examples, this chapter will discuss professional codes of ethics and guide readers to develop an ethical framework for themselves and the organizations they represent.

Simply providing written policies and guidelines without ensuring that people understand and will be held accountable for adhering to them is akin to clicking the "I Agree" box at the end of a lengthy privacy disclosure statement on a software install or signing that you read the patients' privacy information packet at the doctor's office. We've all clicked and/or signed the documents, but have we read the fine print thoroughly each time? I can only speak for myself, but I have not.

Human resources leaders know that one key to any employee development effort is the follow-up measure. Policies and guidelines not only need to be clearly established, but workers also need to understand what they are and how to locate the policies. If an overview of the organization's ethical policies is a mandatory part of new employee orientation, for example, then the written guidelines serve as a reminder of information they have already received. Periodic refreshers in the form of annual, online, self-guided quizzes may also help to reinforce the importance of the policy within the organization.

CASE IN POINT: YOU DECIDE

In a nonprofit development office, new fundraisers should be oriented (and subsequently trained) to understand that donor information is kept highly confidential. If someone wants to make an "anonymous" gift, the organization must determine whether they simply do not want public recognition for their contribution, or whether they want no gift receipt recorded, whatsoever. Having those policies in place in advance helps the organization to properly honor the donor's wishes while maintaining integrity with the information. Oftentimes, even the donor may not realize that there are varying degrees of anonymity, so making ethical guidelines available to constituents is a good learning experience for both parties and builds trust.

Furthermore, breach of confidentiality concerning donor information can be grounds for immediate dismissal and perhaps even felony charges brought against an employee and/or organization for mishandling financial information. These consequences should be made clear at the outset, reiterated, and assessed. As the development manager in this scenario, how would you create an orientation plan to help train new field personnel to handle the complexities of donor anonymity?

Professional codes of ethics lay the foundation for accountability by requiring member organizations to abide by the accepted standards. Outsiders can then make reasonable assumptions about members' principles, based on the best practices identified by the code of ethics. For academic programs in public policy and public administration, NASPAA serves an integral role in holding higher education institutions accountable to the programs within their schools. Across the broader field of public administration, at large, ASPA provides guidelines for public sector agencies to operate within ethical parameters.

NASPAA

Toward the goal of cultivating an inclusive climate among accredited master's programs of public policy and public administration, the Network of Schools of Public Policy, Affairs, and Administration (NASPAA) asserts that graduate students should "... have the ability to deal with incomplete information, complexity, and conflicting demands and be able to reflect upon social and ethical responsibilities linked to the application of their knowledge and judgments."[1] In order to apply knowledge, the information needs to be presented, in the first place. Therefore, NASPAA's *Member Code of Good Practice* suggests that a quality program is one that "integrates ethics into the curriculum and all aspects of program operation, and expects students and faculty to exhibit the highest ethical standards in their teaching, research, and service."[2] A key aim of this text, in fact, is to accomplish just that: to weave ethics within the fiscal administration curriculum and provide opportunities (through case study discussions) for students to apply content knowledge in a practical, real-world manner.

Among the four preconditions required for accreditation review, NASPAA's list of standards for master's degree programs includes a section titled Public Service Values:

> Public service values are important and enduring beliefs, ideals and principles shared by members of a community about what is good and desirable and what is not. They include pursuing the public interest with accountability and transparency; serving professionally with competence, efficiency, and objectivity; acting ethically so as to uphold the public trust; and demonstrating respect, equity, and fairness in dealings with citizens and fellow public servants.[3]

As we will discuss further in this chapter, NASPAA's emphasis on serving the public interest, first and foremost, is a key component in developing an ethical framework to guide fiscal administrators. Graduate programs would do well to place a deliberate focus on cultivating these values among their students.

ASPA

The American Society for Public Administration (ASPA) has incorporated ethics into its strategic plan, with a stated goal to "advocate strong, effective and ethical public governance."[4] To further illustrate the organization's commitment to these issues, ASPA's Code of Ethics[5] provides eight points of guidance for public and nonprofit sector agencies. Among these standards is a call to "advance the public interest." In keeping with the prevailing notion of public service, organizations are urged to put one's own interests on the back burner in deference to the interests of the public.

The ASPA Code of Ethics also includes aspects of transparency, participation, and collaboration, three goals that we will find to be recurring themes throughout this chapter. For example, ASPA encourages public sector agencies to "promote democratic participation." This guideline goes hand-in-hand with communication and transparency, as organizations seek to serve all of their constituents respectfully and inclusively. Another standard that ASPA notes is to "fully inform and advise" both internal and external stakeholders.[6] Again, this hearkens to a commitment of open communication. The organization also challenges public sector leaders to "demonstrate personal integrity" while they "promote ethical organizations." These two principles reinforce the need for public administrators to lead by example through upstanding professional behavior and accept no less from their respective organizations.

Developing an Ethical Framework

Understanding an agency's legal obligations concerning accounting and reporting practices is important, but as we mentioned at the beginning of this text, many of the day-to-day decisions that public fiscal administrators face are not newsworthy (at least, we hope not!). However, some of those discretionary choices may have long-term consequences for the organization and require thoughtful analysis prior to implementing. In order to guide public budget managers logically through this decision making process, we will create an ethical framework, starting with a nod to Corporate Social Responsibility as a relevant example from the private sector, as well as incorporating the three pillars of the Open Government Directive: transparency, participation, and collaboration.

Corporate Social Responsibility as an Example

Although the private sector exists to make a profit, advocates of ethical responsibility hold that corporations also have altruistic duties, including philanthropic activities and public policy advocacy. This notion of establishing corporate citizenship by combining a positive societal reputation with competitive business advantage is dubbed Corporate Social Responsibility. Put another way, CSR can be defined as "any concept concerning how managers should handle public policy and social issues."[7]

Rather than focus solely on economic stakeholders, CSR proponents view society as the primary stakeholder of their business operations. This relationship can manifest in terms of strategic philanthropic contributions to charitable organizations, or even lobbying for public policy changes that would benefit society beyond the self-interests of the corporation. Returning to the public sector, then, we would do well to borrow certain aspects of CSR in developing our ethical framework for public fiscal administration. By keeping society in mind as the primary stakeholder of our efforts, the focus of our work will stay centered on fulfilling the mission and vision of our respective agencies and organizations.

Imagine that you are planning a cross-country road trip using online maps. When you plot the course from Point A to Point B, the mapping tool will likely offer several options about which roads to take. In fact, you might purposely add stops along the way, such as scheduling a detour to visit a National Park or other tourist attraction. You might avoid toll roads or freeways, preferring to take a more scenic route. Or, perhaps time is of the essence, and you look for the route with the fastest speed limits and fewest construction zones. The destination is set, but how you get there may vary widely.

As with CSR, the focus of public administration, as a practice, should be serving the public. However, the way in which your local Department of Motor Vehicles goes about achieving that end game will look different from the methods the Division of Wildlife Resources takes. Regardless of the agency or level of government, we can use a logic model[8] as a guide to address the three pillars of transparency, participation, and collaboration. For each pillar, we will consider six components:

1. **Purpose:** First and foremost, it is important to know the purpose, or mission, of your organization. What is your agency's mission statement? Everything we do from this point forward should be grounded in the mission. If there is a need for change, then proposed alternatives should reflect back on the mission statement.

2. **Context:** Budgetary decisions do not occur in a vacuum; we must be mindful of the conditions in which our agencies operate. Economies flourish and flounder based on the actions of investors and consumers. Likewise, governmental systems ebb and flow on an undercurrent of political opinion. Ask yourself: Are there political changes in the works that are affecting the climate of our organization? What is the current state of the economy, and are there any recent fiscal challenges that we need to be aware of? Are there competing organizations – both private and nonprofit – that serve the same target audience and may put our funding in jeopardy?

3. **Inputs:** What resources do we have on hand to fulfill the organization's mission? Are we solely reliant on one source of revenue, or do we have a variety of income streams from which to draw? What options do we have to diversify our revenue sources? Are there constraints that we need to bear in mind with existing revenue pools, such as guidelines concerning grant funds?

4. **Activities:** What will our organization or agency do, tangibly, to achieve its goals? What pros and cons do we need to consider with our proposed next steps?

5. **Outputs:** How will we know that what we've set out to do actually worked to bring our organization further along in its mission? What performance measures will we establish to document our successes?

6. **Effects:** What do we envision to be the long-term results of our efforts? What specific consequences do we hope to observe? What type of direct impact will we have on our target population? What about indirect influences on the surrounding community, partner agencies, policy development, etc.?

As noted above, the practice of public administration will manifest in different activities and outcomes, depending on the type of agency, scope of services, level of government, and a myriad of other factors. The focus of this particular text is on ethical fiscal management; however, the framework may be adapted and applied to a variety of public administration goals. Therefore, this framework is designed to be a flexible shell, not a blueprint with every step clearly labeled. One important aspect that public and nonprofit sector agencies and organizations share in common, however, is an underlying commitment to serving the public. Now that we have identified the components of our logic model, we will continue building our ethical framework by applying these six elements to the three pillars of the Open Government Directive (discussed previously in Chapter 7): transparency, participation, and collaboration.

Transparency

1. As it is currently drafted, does the agency's mission encourage inclusiveness and public accountability? How could we incorporate transparency in keeping with the overall vision of the organization?
2. What is the current climate surrounding our organization, in terms of transparency? What are we doing to publicize the good things that our agency is accomplishing?
3. Is our budget process open to public observation? For taxing agencies: Do we make the public aware of how their tax dollars are being used? For nonprofit organizations: How well do we steward our donors and keep them informed of how their charitable contributions are being put to use?
4. How well does the public understand what we actually do, as an agency or organization? Is our website easily navigable and informative? Is external communication a priority?
5. Are our goals in sync with the public's expectations of our agency or organization? In other words, when we view our work as successful, is the public on the same page? Does the public understand what our agency does financially, in terms of how much we collect and spend to accomplish those goals?
6. Thinking ahead five years from now, what would make you truly proud to work for this agency? What would it look like for the public to appreciate the efforts of the organization?

CASE IN POINT: YOU DECIDE

Due to their charters as entities of the state, public universities' budgets are available for public access and viewing. The process of developing said budgets, however, may not always be open and inclusive. Too often, budgetary decisions are made by a handful of individuals with little to no input from internal or external stakeholders. Some universities, however, are taking proactive measures to turn the tide by inviting input from faculty and staff, as well as presenting public hearings as part of the budget development process.

If you represented the budget office at a public university, how might you encourage the administration to make its budget preparation process more transparent and inclusive? How would you respond to push-back from naysayers who suggest that a more participatory process would unduly drag out an already laborious, time-consuming endeavor?

Participation

1. If public involvement is not already part of our mission statement, what can the organization do to encourage greater participation?
2. How would you describe current public opinion concerning the organization? Do people perceive our agency as efficient and valuable, or does it have a reputation for being wasteful and full of red tape?
3. Is the public aware of the needs of the organization? Do we include representatives from the public in strategic planning and/or fundraising?
4. Do we offer means for public input into our agency's daily activities? Such feedback could be in the form of online satisfaction surveys, comment boxes in the office, a "Contact Us" portal on the website, etc.
5. Whether it is through town hall-style meetings, a public relations campaign, press release, or other mode, how are we involving the public in celebrating the accomplishments of our organization? Depending on the agency, are there success stories of clients that we can share?
6. What would look different about our organization if we were to become more participatory? Is there common agreement about what the term *participatory* means, as it pertains to our work?

Collaboration

1. Does the agency's mission encourage collaboration internally between employees and board members, employees and other employees, etc.? What association do we have, if any, with sister agencies or organizations? How could strengthening such relationships help to fulfill our purpose as an organization?
2. Is there a spirit of cooperation or teamwork within our agency and the larger community? What obstacles might be hindering us from developing partnerships with other groups?
3. Are budgetary decisions and strategic planning the work of a handful of insiders, or is the process collaborative and welcome to input from others? To what extent are decisions seen as secretive or the product of a concerted effort?
4. Do we have a community advisory board to provide insight into the organization's needs and goals? How do we involve internal and external stakeholders to participate in the activities of the organization?
5. Are successes celebrated, and if so, does the organization engage the community and other external stakeholders?
6. What would the budget planning process look like if our agency approached decision-making with a collaborative perspective? Are there areas in which our organization has functioned in silos that could be opened to fresh input?

By reviewing both routine and unusual budgetary decisions through the lenses of transparency, participation, and collaboration, we will develop public and nonprofit sector organizations that are built on an ethical, mission-minded foundation. Granted, not every decision will be black-and-white with clear answers; however, the questions embedded in the framework above are designed to help public fiscal administrators navigate the what-ifs and come to a decision that works in the best interest of the organization's mission.

Conclusion

When we consider the historical underpinnings of public administration in the United States, from Alexander Hamilton's inclination toward organizational structure and Max Weber's prioritization of efficiency to Woodrow Wilson's formalization of the public sector, we can see that decision making concerning the public interest has always included a measure of ethical philosophy. The foundation of natural law and the evolution of a social contract theory implied that the public ought to have a voice in the construct of its governing bodies. As time has marched on, we see increased emphasis placed on transparency, participation, and collaboration within government agencies, as well as the public and nonprofit sectors at large.

We looked at the role of government, failures of the market, and elements from private business that we can apply to public sector finance. Political influences on the budget process led to our conversation on public administrators as moral agents, as well as obligations of the nonprofit sector to abide by similarly high standards of integrity. After examining reporting and accounting standards, we considered the need to innovate and adapt to technological change in a manner that fulfills ethical expectations. Finally, we explored professional codes of conduct and broke down the three pillars of transparency, participation, and collaboration to design our own ethical framework for public and nonprofit administrators.

A key goal in crafting this text was to help fiscal administrators understand that managing public resources means a lot more than being able to navigate spreadsheets. It is important to understand the history of public administration and ascertain how political winds influence the way budgetary decisions are made. Ethical fiscal administrators need to be able to think about both the short- and long-term ramifications of their decisions, beyond figures on a page. To borrow a quote from W. E. Deming in the private sector, "He that would run his company on visible figures alone will in time have neither company nor figures."[9] Upholding the public trust is a substantial challenge, and public administration is a noble field.

Notes

1 *Creating an Inclusive Climate.* Retrieved from: accreditation.naspaa.org/resources/diversity-resources/building-an-inclusive-program.

2 *NASPAA Member Code of Good Practice*. Retrieved from: www.naspaa.org/about_na spaa/members/code.
3 *NASPAA Preconditions for Accreditation Review*, 2. Retrieved from: naspaaaccreditation. files.wordpress.com/2015/02/naspaa-accreditation-standards.pdf.
4 ASPA 2015–16 Strategic Plan, Goal 1. Retrieved from: www.aspanet.org/ASPA/ About-ASPA/Governance/ASPA/About-ASPA/Governance/Governance.aspx?hkey= 00114468-5e85-4c18-bde0-62bbdf067651.
5 *ASPA Code of Ethics*. Retrieved from: www.aspanet.org/ASPA/Code-of-Ethics/ASPA/ Code-of-Ethics/Code-of-Ethics.aspx?hkey=5b8f046b-dcbd-416d-87cd-0b8fcfacb5e7.
6 Ibid.
7 Windsor, D. (2006). Corporate Social Responsibility: Three Key Approaches. *The Journal of Management Studies, 43*(1): 93–114.
8 For more information on developing a logic model, visit the Community Tool Box at ctb.ku.edu/en/table-of-contents/overview/models-for-community-health-and-deve lopment/logic-model-development/main. The Community Tool Box is a service of the Work Group for Community Health and Development at the University of Kansas.
9 Deming, W. E. (2000). *Out of the Crisis*. Cambridge, MA: MIT Press, 121.

INDEX

Made in the USA
Las Vegas, NV
28 August 2021

29172336R00105